THE
PARABLES OF JESUS

THE
PARABLES OF JESUS

By the Right Reverend
COSMO GORDON LANG, D.D., D.C.L.
Archbishop of York

NEW AMERICAN EDITION

NEW YORK
E. P. DUTTON & COMPANY
681 Fifth Avenue

NEW AMERICAN EDITION
APRIL, 1918

Printed in the United States of America

TO

MY FATHER AND MOTHER

PREFACE

The following papers were written in response to many requests from those who had read my former very unpretentious volume on "The Miracles of Jesus," and who wished to have some of the Parables treated in a similar manner. Like the papers on the Miracles, they were originally published month by month in *Good Words;* like them, they were written under great difficulties and in the midst of other pressing work. They are, therefore, inevitably marked by the same obvious shortcomings. I hope that they may be read separately rather than as chapters in a consecutive book.

It would be mere presumption to attempt to write anything on the subject of the Parables without using the guidance of Archbishop Trench's scholarship and insight; but I have thought it best not to consult any other commentaries.

C. G. L.

Amen Court,
S. Paul's Cathedral,
November, 1905.

CONTENTS

CONTENTS

THE USE OF PARABLES IN THE
TEACHING OF JESUS

THE USE OF PARABLES IN THE TEACHING OF JESUS

THE use of parables was the special mark of Jesus' popular teaching — "without a parable spake He not unto them." It is easy to see the fitness of this kind of teaching (1) It was a method to which His hearers were accustomed. Orientals are born story-tellers; their common speech is proverbial and parabolic. Teaching otherwise clothed would have been unreal, inaccessible to them. Our Lord when He came among men came not outwardly as a marvel, but as a brother, moving freely among the people with whom He lived and of whom, "as concerning the flesh," He came, using their customary ways of thinking and speaking. He taught men in their own language; taught as a Rabbi, differing from other Rabbis, not in His method, but in the originality, the force, the strange and compelling authority which He showed in His use of it. (2) It was a method which arrested attention. You must always have clear in your imagination the scene of each parable—the Teacher standing there with the burden of truth upon His heart, and the crowd before Him; and remember what a crowd of men, a thing always so wonderful must have meant to the Son of Man. Well, He must make them listen. With the sympathy and earnestness of the true Teacher He would swiftly and spontaneously use the suggestions of the moment—things passing before the eyes of His audience, familiar in their daily life, the ways of husbandman and housewife, the tales and news of the countryside—and thus catch and keep their attention. (3) It was a method which aroused thought. The great Teacher knew that He could not teach His hearers unless He made them teach themselves. He must reach their own minds and get *them* to work with His. The *form* of the parable would attract all; but only the thoughtful could read its meaning. It could not be found without thinking. The parables therefore both attracted and sifted the crowd. Those only who "had ears" could hear—those only who were in earnest would either care or come to understand. (4) Hence it was a method which preserved the truth. What men think out for themselves they never forget; the exercise of their mind makes it their own. Moreover the language of symbols— expressed in what is seen by the eye or pictured by the imagination — is more powerful and enduring in its effects than the language of mere abstract words. It conveys and brings back to the mind the inner meaning with swiftness and sureness; it carries with it a wealth of suggestion and association. And mere words are constantly changing their meaning, whereas the symbols of Life and Nature such as our Lord used in His parables are as abiding as Nature and Life themselves.

Among all the teachers who have used this method of teaching, Jesus stands unrivalled. There is nothing in literature which can be compared with His parables. How familiar they are, yet how everlastingly fresh! Interwoven with all the memories of our lives, wrought into the texture of our daily speech, they yet retain a force and vividness wholly their own. So simple in form that a child may understand them, they are yet so deep in meaning that Christian thought for nearly two thousand years has pondered over them without exhausting their treasures. The criticism of the Gospels, historical and literary, which has in so many ways changed and disturbed (as well as deepened) our knowledge of the life and words of Christ, leaves these stories for the most part untouched. No one can doubt that in studying them we are quite literally studying the very words of Jesus. They bear the mark of personality, the stamp of unique and incommunicable genius. They bring us to Him who spoke as man has never spoken.

From these thoughts two principles spring which shall guide our study. The first is, we must remember that each parable was spoken not primarily to unborn generations, but to living groups of bystanders and disciples. It had a single special lesson, meant for them, which they could understand. That primary lesson must always be our first concern. It must remain the touchstone of the worth of all our own interpretations. They must be consistent with it. No detail must be pressed to teach something plainly outside its limits. Thus (to quote familiar and egregious instances of a method only too common in all ages of Christian teaching) to see in some of the details of the story of the Good Samaritan a proof of the order of process in the Fall of Man, and an anticipation of the institution of the two great sacraments; to look upon the story of the Unjust Steward as a history of the apostasy of Satan; to discern in the Pearl of Great Price a description of the Church of Geneva—this is to ignore the unity of meaning given by our Lord Himself in the im-

mediate lesson which He was impressing on
His immediate audience, and to make interpretation fanciful, artificial, even violent.
On the other hand—and this is our second
principle of study—He who spoke these
parables was the Son of God and the Son of
Man—the Word of God incarnate. However simple His words may have been they
had in them the width and depth of the
Truth itself. We shall therefore expect that
the main lesson of each parable will carry
us far, if we have power to follow it, into
the deep things of life and God—nay, that
the details will possess in relation to this
main lesson a significance of their own. The
parables will soon lead us to the mysteries of
the Kingdom of God. We may even see "a
mystery" in the very use of the parables by
the Word Incarnate—the truth, namely,
that the connection between the parable and
the lesson is not merely accidental; that it
corresponds to some inner harmony of
thought and things. I cannot do better than
quote the words of Archbishop Trench
(whose introduction to the study of the

parables in spite of the lapse of years since it was written remains unique, full of scholarship, insight and beauty) : "This entire moral and visible world from first to last, with its kings and its subjects, its parents and its children, its sun and its moon, its sowing and its harvest, its light and its darkness, its sleeping and its waking, its birth and its death, is from beginning to end a mighty parable, a great teaching of supersensuous truth . . . Christ moved in the midst of what seemed to the eye of sense an old and worn-out world, and it evidently became new at His touch; for it told to man *now* the inmost secrets of his being, answered with strange and marvellous correspondences to another world within him, helped to the birth great thoughts of his heart, which before were helplessly struggling to be born—these two worlds, without him and within, each throwing a light and a glory on the other."

Jesus was man and God; His parables were simple, suited to the men He met on earth, yet were they also glimpses of truth

deep and divine. May the Holy Spirit of
God, the Giver of Life, through our study
of them, make these venerable stories of
Jesus live anew in our minds and lives!

THE SOWER

THE SOWER

S. Matt. xiii. 3-8, 18-23; *S. Mark* iv. 3-8, 14-20;
S. Luke viii. 5-8, 11-15

I. THE SEED IS THE WORD

WE begin with the great Parable of the
Sower. It is the story with which Jesus
Himself seems to have ushered His parabolic method of teaching. It is the one
which He gave as a type of all the rest, and
concerning which He laid down the reasons
which led Him to choose this way of reaching the hearts and consciences of His
hearers. It is easy for us to imagine the
scene of its first telling. Around the Master
were the blue waters of the lake; before
Him, on the fringe of bright yellow sand,
stood the crowd of Eastern peasants, eager

to hear the new Teacher, so unlike the
formal and precise Rabbis to whom they
were accustomed, as He sat there in the
freshness and freedom of the open air. It
may be that as he raised His glance, it fell
upon some countryman on the slope of the
hill behind the beach, sowing his seed, the
birds flying around and behind him. That
sight interpreted to Jesus with swift vivid
reality His own immediate situation—His
presence there, meeting His brother men,
with the message of their Father on His
lips, the love of their Father in His heart;
these faces before Him, each of them repre-
senting some separate story of toil, of love,
of hope, of need, of sorrow. "Behold! the
sower went forth to sow."

How could He make the words which
came from His own very life become the
germs of new and satisfying life in all these
waiting folk? He knew that all depended
upon the receptivity of the soil—on the dis-
position of the heart and mind. At the out-
set of our study of the parables, let us lay to
heart that first and essential lesson. We shall

make no progress in this or any other branch of Christian learning until we have grasped it. The Divine Teacher requires the right correspondence of heart and will. Truth cannot be known, grace cannot be received, without the fitting response of character. The message of Christian truth will never prove itself, the gift of Christian grace will never fulfil itself. To understand the first and to use the second really and vitally, a man must put and keep himself in the right attitude of mind and will. The object of the parable is to tell us what that right attitude is.

The seed is "the word," "the word of God," "the word of the Kingdom." The sower is the Living Spirit of God who breathes the word. The Spirit, like the wind, blows where He lists; and every breath of that Divine Spirit is a word of God. The language in which He speaks is manifold, unexpected, all-pervading as Himself. Whenever the spirit of a man is touched and aroused, a word of God has been spoken. Sometimes it is spoken

through Nature in the glory of the setting
sun, in the plash of the waters upon the
shore, in the shapes and shadows of great
mountains, in the multitude and silence of
the stars, in the stillness of the "huge and
thoughtful night." Sometimes the word is
spoken through human lives—as when the
example of a true man or woman warms the
heart and fires the will, or when some spectacle of suffering quickens the instinct of
compassion. Sometimes the word is spoken
through memories of days and faces gone,
through old associations rousing remorse, or
reviving forgotten hopes. Sometimes it is
spoken when some chord of music stirs
strange yearnings in the soul and inarticu-
late "thoughts too deep for tears." Sometimes it speaks again to our own spirits with
some echo of the power or pleading with
which centuries ago it first sounded in the
spirit of God's chosen men, when we read
and hear the venerable words of the Bible.
Has the inner spirit of a man at any time
and in any way been reached and drawn towards good and God?—Then and there

God has been speaking to him. Once indeed
the Spirit of God expressed Himself in a
Perfect Word—in *the* Word of God incarnate; and still the surest sign which a man
can have that God Himself is speaking to
Him is when the thought of Jesus moves
him to grateful reverence, the example of
Jesus inspires him to the service of his fellows, the Spirit of Jesus gives him the
ardour of hope, and the strength of life. In
all these manifold ways the Spirit of God
is ceaselessly speaking divine words—the
Sower is ever going forth to sow.

Whether or not these words of God enter
within us as life-giving seeds, springing up
in healthy and progressive life, and bearing
fruit, depends upon the quality of the soil.
It is this which we have to examine and
prepare. This is the essential "spade
work" of the Christian life.

II. THE WAYSIDE SOIL

Some seed fell upon the *wayside soil*.
On the pathway trodden hard by the feet

of men, the scattered seed finds no entry.
It lies upon the surface, and the birds
which fly in the wake of the sower pick it
up and carry it away. The wayside soil
is the type of the hardened heart. (1) The
heart is hardened often by the routine of
daily life, monotonous and persistent. Work
we must have; hard work it is well for us
to have; but if work is to ennoble and not
enslave, the inner spirit of the worker must
be kept free, otherwise the whole life is
pressed down, becomes hard and flat,
narrow and barren. You remember that
epitaph, so significant of the common failures of life, "Born a man, he died a grocer."
"The daily round, the common task," are
indeed "a road to bring us daily nearer
God." But they are this only when the
road is continually broken up by the free
movement of His Spirit. There are three
simple ways of preventing this hardening
of the heart by the routine of life. One is
Prayer. It is busy, hard-working men who
have most need of the daily prayer. The
habit of prayer keeps the character moist

with the dews of heaven, open and responsive to the seed-words of God. The second
is the right observance of the weekly
Sabbath—the rest for recreation: the pause,
regularly enforced in the pressure of work,
in which a man makes time to remember
the Lord his God, and in the worship of
the Church to enter another and a higher
world. And these two are in close connection. For—

> "Every day should leave some part
> Free for a Sabbath of the heart:
> So shall the seventh be truly blest
> From morn to eve with hallowed rest."

The third is the momentary recollection
of God in the midst of daily work—as it is
quaintly called, "the practice of the Presence
of God." You remember one Brother
Lawrence, the monastery cook, who in the
duties of the kitchen, by this means
"possessed God in tranquillity." These
momentary upliftings of the soul to God,
in shop and factory, in street and railway,
keep the soil from hardening and make it
responsive to the words of God.

(2) The heart is often hardened by the familiarity of religious language. The accustomed phrases fall on our ears or rise to our lips with dangerous facility. Unless they are constantly questioned and tested, they become a mere hardening patter of words. You have sung that hymn—you have heard that sentence in a sermon— you have used these phrases in your family prayers. Ask: "What does this really mean to me?" It is often a good thing to think quietly for five minutes about the tremendous import of the simplest phrases of religion. "From all hardness of heart and contempt of Thy word and commandment, good Lord, deliver us."

III. THE THIN-SURFACED SOIL

Some seed fell upon the *thin-surfaced soil*. Where there is a mere layer of earth covering a hard rock, the seed cannot spread downwards and take strong root,

and its growth is both sudden and short-
lived. "Those on the rock are they which
when they have heard receive the word
with joy; and these have no root, which
for a while believe and in time of temptation fall away." In the pregnant phrase
of S. Luke, "they have no root in themselves." Alas! there is here for very many
of us the need of anxious self-testing. Has
our religion any real root in ourselves? It
may be that our religious emotions are quick
and warm; that our interest in religious or
ecclesiastical matters is intense. It may
be that we have even gone through, to us,
memorable religious experiences. All these
things are good in their own way; but they
are only surface matters. The Word of God
can find no soil in which to take root there.
It must get down to a man's *will;* for his
inner self is what he is *willing* to be. Unless
religion is conceived as *an obligation*—a
power which reaches, grasps, and holds the
will—it cannot stand the strain of life.

There comes perhaps the temptation to
grow tired of moral drudgery—the long

and weary task of daily self-discipline, of clearing out some besetting fault. It is tedious and depressing, assuredly; and the feelings of religion can apparently maintain themselves without it; why take so much pains about it? Yet it is scarcely too much to say that two-thirds of true practical religion is just this drudgery of daily discipline. I am convinced it can only be faced, maintained, brought out to success by a man whose religion has got down to the roots of his being, and there more and more works with the steadiness and spontaneity of a new instinct.

There comes perhaps the trial of a great sorrow. Ah, how common, how pitiful, is the spectacle of the withering of religion under the blight of suffering! "I used to enjoy my prayers; I loved my church, its sacraments, its services; and now, just when I want it most, my religion fails me." Many a time have I heard that bitter complaint on the lips of those who, when the sun shone, were very religious. Doubtless it may be failure of nerves rather than failure of faith which accounts for this sense of blankness. But too often the reason is that faith has not got down to and mingled itself with the roots of life—its elementary instincts, its enduring characteristics. How different these complaints from the words with which Jesus, in whom the Father's will was the very breath of life, met the coming of His Passion — "Father, the hour is come, glorify Thy Son."

Or there may come the trial of "persecution." We may be sure that our religion has only a surface hold when we find that it becomes harassed, petulant, distressed in the atmosphere of criticism; and criticism is the most common modern substitute for the older and franker modes of persecution. If a man's religion is part of himself—rooted in the bases of his being—he will not be tossed to and fro by the currents of opinion and talk. He may not be able to meet argument by argument, he may be baffled often in his own reasoning, but the "man in him," the real self, will remain unshaken. That is the lesson for our learning.

Religion, if it is to be sure and strong, must be pressed down till it reaches and grasps a man's inmost self—that self which abides the same beneath all changes and chances of life and sorrow and doubt. This is the *radical* reform of which the characters of most of us stand in urgent need. It comes to this—have we any conviction for which we are ready to die, *i. e.,* which we could not give up without giving up the whole meaning of life? Such a final standing-ground Frederic Robertson reached. "In the darkest hours through which a human soul can pass, whatever else is doubtful, this at least is certain—if there is no God, no future state, yet even then it is better to be generous than selfish, better to be true than false, better to be brave than to be a coward." Not much, you may say, but at least it was a root which had wrought itself into the fibres of the man's whole being. Therefore a new strong faith could grow up from it—"a faith and hope and trust," as he says, "no longer traditional but his own —a trust which neither earth nor hell shall shake henceforth for ever." Such a standing-ground they reach who know that they would rather part with life itself than with the conviction which alone to them gives life its meaning and its inspiration, the conviction that the inner voice which once called them from the drift of indifference and set the light of a true ideal before them, and since then has cheered and guided them in their new journey was the voice of a Living Person, Jesus the Lord and Brother of men. Rest not satisfied till you have found some such holding root of faith. Plant it deep in the bases of your life. Test its strength by its control over the will. Do not despise, but distrust mere feeling; and look to *acts* as the real proof of your religion. For it is by action, more and more immediate and instinctive and quick to obey the promptings of faith, that the fibres of faith's root become entwined close and strong around your inmost self. It is from a religon thus deep-rooted that a man's character brings forth a harvest for God's gathering.

IV. THE CHOKED SOIL

Again, there is the *choked soil*—the soil in which the alien growths of the cares and pleasures of life choke and strangle the growth of God's seed.

"Other seed fell amidst the thorns: and the thorns grew with it and choked it." "These are they that have heard and as they go on their way they are choked with cares and riches and pleasures of this life, and bring no fruit to perfection" (S. Luke vii. 7, 114). Here, you will notice, the fault is not with the soil itself: it has great possibilities: it is rich and deep enough, but it wants weeding. It wastes its strength in nourishing the weeds. It is not enough that the seed should find a root: it must have *room to grow*.

(1) It is very noteworthy that our Lord expressly puts "the care of this world," "the care of this life," among the thorns which strangle the growth of the true life, By "care" He means, not quiet and

purposeful thought, but that division of the
heart (such is the force of the Greek word),
that over-pressing anxiety, that fretting,
which exhausts the energies of life.   How
hard it is for any "fruits of the Spirit" to
grow up in the midst of this fretting care
any knowledge of the lives of the masses of
our labouring folk abundantly shows. I do
not think I can do better than quote the
following words from the recent striking
charge of the Bishop of Southwark (then
Bishop of Rochester).* "The great French
preacher, Lacordaire, discussing the salvation of the many or the few, declared that
the great mass of mankind would find their
salvation through toil. But there is another
side to the matter; the sociologist will also
tell you that compulsory exertion in the
form of excessive and protracted labour
blunts and stunts all the faculties—and our
appeal is to one of the most sensitive and
delicate of these faculties—man's moral and
spiritual sense. . . . When we have made

* "The Church's Failure and the Work of Christ,"
p. 24.

the most of the blessings of drudgery and of
occupied hands, we must still feel that this
heavy mechanical overstrain of task-work
yields but little of that which should
quicken and instruct the best interests of
man and draw his heart to God." No one
can doubt that the patience, the cheerfulness, the neighbourliness of the hard-working poor betoken a true and rich soil of
human nature, but its capacities are strained
and exhausted by this all-compelling "care."
I was much struck by the remark made to
me not long ago by a good working-man—
"You wonder why the likes of me take so
little thought for religion. Well, the fact
is, we are mostly tired out." The good soil
is "tired out": it becomes incapable of
moral and spiritual effort. The energies of
the soul cannot stand the double strain.
Every effort, therefore, to lighten the pressure of toil, to make work more interesting
in itself, shorter in its duration, more assured of its wage, makes for religion.

And yet it remains true that the Gospel is
very specially meant for tired folk, for the

weary and heavy laden. It is to them a
gift of rest—the rest, the freedom from fret,
which comes with a tranquil trust in the
constant love of God. By that trust the
spirit rises to the calm of the Divine Will;
it is there refreshed and strengthened, and
thence it returns to the toil and spreads its
own tranquillity over it. Trust in God's
care takes the care which is anxious out of
the heart of toil,—"casting all your care
upon Him for He careth for you." That
patience which is always pathetic becomes
in God's servants—have we not often seen
it?—a certain heroic serenity: it speaks of
triumph rather than endurance, of mastery
rather than submission. The toil of a man
whose spirit rises to God and keeps hold on
Him becomes a discipline which helps, not
a "care" which strangles, the growth of the
soul. I am sure that we all, whatever our
life task may be, have need of renewing that
primary faith in the reality of Providence.
The simplicity which really trusts and acts
upon the truth that life is ordered by the
Will of God always brings with it calmness

and strength. "Sit down" said Carlyle's
father to his sons who rose from the family
prayers, when a gust of wind shook the
cottage, to protect the stacks of corn—"sit
down: there cannot a straw be touched but
by the Will of God." A simple faith, no
doubt, and perhaps crudely expressed, but
the faith by which the "still, strong man"
is made.

(2) "The deceitfulness of riches," "the
pleasures of this life"—these also choke the
seeds of God. There is even more danger
in the pursuit of wealth and pleasure than
in the compulsion of toil. Not even the
large-hearted Lacordaire could say that
some men could be saved by their comforts
or their amusements. The soul is more
prone to be atrophied by comfort than to
be worn out by toil. Any honest self-
scrutiny shows most of us plainly enough
the astonishing subtlety and closeness with
which the little comforts of life entangle the
spirit. They are innocent in themselves, so
that we are put off our guard, but in the
bulk they are very Delilah's cords, and

when the spirit is called to make some effort
or sacrifice it finds itself tied and bound.
"Come, follow me."—"When he heard this
he was very sorrowful for he was very rich."
We know not when or how the summons
may come to test the strength and freedom
of the spirit: let us prepare for it by preventing these comforts of life from becoming its masters. Let us keep the upper hand
over them by deliberate acts of self-denial;
use them, as those who are ready at any
moment to dispense with them. It is sadly
true that "vocations are missed daily"
through mere softness of living. The spirit
cannot work its way through the network
of comforts which have been allowed to become indispensable. You do not accuse a
gardener of spoiling his garden because he
does some weeding every day. Neither do
we spoil or thwart life by deliberate rules
of self-discipline. We only strengthen it and
maintain its freedom, give room in it for
the seeds of the spirit to grow.

I have not spoken of the more absorbing
"pleasures of this life." It is enough

simply to say that it is sternly impossible
for that large class which exists to amuse
itself and makes pleasure its all-engrossing
business to "save" its soul. Is it too much
to say that the Thames on a Sunday after-
noon would be to any eyes which knew the
truth about human life and its destiny an
infinitely more pitiful sight than a dingy
street crowded with white and worn
toilers?

(3) But there is a phrase in S. Mark's
version of the parable which perhaps comes
nearer to the conscience of most of us. The
seed is choked by "the lusts of other
things entering in"—"The lusts of other
things"—the jostle of all sorts of desires and
impulses. Is it not a phrase descriptive of
a type of character very common in these
days? They are days of perpetual movement, distraction, dissipation of thought and
energy. Modern character takes its hue
from this environment. I saw the other day
a bill on a music-hall door, "Lightning
changes: programme constantly varied." It
seemed a faithful caricature of our modern

life—so hurried, so distracted by a thousand influences of newspapers, magazines, opinions, all of which find some response within us. There is, indeed, a very real craving for religion—the very restlessness of men brings a desire for faith, their very nervousness becomes a plea for rest. But these promptings of the true spirit, the reaching forth of the real needs of the soul, are choked by the medley of manifold influences and dissipated desires. The prophet's warning to our day and generation—indeed, to ourselves, for we are all influenced by the spirit of the time—must be not only "Repent," but also very specially *"Simplify your life."* Go thinning in the garden of your soul; select the plants which you mean to grow: there is no room for all. If we are to be Christians it must be, not by custom or even by mere desire and aspiration, but by the deliberate choice of the will. We must *choose* which of the contending claims of business, pleasure, society, ambition, Christ, we mean in the last resort to prevail. There is no other way of success.

If we are content with these over-crowded characters we shall "bring no fruit to perfection." If we try to keep both pleasure and Christ as our main motives of living, we shall lose both. Those who are able to learn moral truth through striking paradox might read, on this stern law of life, Browning's "Statue and the Bust" or Kipling's "Tomlinson." The one quite certain way of spoiling life is the way of the divided will. It is really not worth while to have a half-hearted religion, for a half-hearted religion (as we shall shall learn from another parable) spoils not only the service of God but also the service of mammon. We cannot hope our religion to be either a joy to ourselves or a help to others unless and until we have settled once for all that the Master who has the right of the last word in all debates of duty or desire is not self, or the world, but Christ. So far as it rests with us to make our religion a happiness and a power the one thing needful is single-heart and sincere choice of it as the supreme rule of life.

V. THE GOOD SOIL

For this, says our Lord, is *the good soil*. "That on the good ground are they which in an honest and good heart, having heard the word, keep it and bring forth fruit with patience." "An honest and good heart." After all that we have said we are not surprised at the extreme simplicity of this description. To be really sincere towards God—that is the great need. Honesty and goodness of heart—given these conditions in the soil, the Spirit of God can rear His seeds. These were the conditions which Jesus sought in His first disciples. For the most part, they were simple, honest, open-air men—life the fishermen on our own coasts, who look at us with straight eyes and speak to us with straight words. He knew that in their frankness and simplicity He had the capacity for response. So He could do in them and through them whatsoever He wished. How often we have known gifted but complicated characters,

who interested us, perhaps fascinated us,
but who disappointed us because we saw in
them no progress; and on the other hand,
simple men with honest hearts, touched by
the grace of God, who moved straight on in
tranquil strength. *"Honesty"*: we are to be
simply honest in the things of religion. It
was Newman who said that the man who
was wholly honest was already perfect. For
if a man is really and truly surrendered to
the Divine Will, so that his whole nature is
expressed in the prayer, "Speak Lord for
Thy servant heareth," "Here am I, send
me," then the Spirit of God has free course
within him. *"Goodness"*: we are to have a
great ambition to be "good," to hate and
despise as by a strong instinct all mean-
nesses, inconsistencies, jealousies; to be as
self-less and absorbed in the quest of goodness as the child is in his play. For what
is this honesty and goodness of heart but
the spirit of the child? We are always
brought back to that great condition of
entry into the Kingdom of God—"be con-
verted and become as little children." In

proportion as we are thus open to the Spirit of God we shall grow—grow gradually towards the likeness of Christ. It is for God to choose how full the growth shall be, how rich in the graces of character, in the power of influence—"some an hundred fold, some sixty fold, some thirty fold." It is enough that we oppose no obstacle to His spirit. He will bring forth the fruit in due season.

Lord, I am nothing in myself: my worth is only what Thou canst make me to be. Make me to love what Thou lovest, will what Thou willest, desire what Thou desirest, serve where Thou sendest, be ready when Thou callest.

If such a prayer come from the heart, as the expression of real purpose and desire, the heart from which it comes is the good soil.

THE MUSTARD SEED AND THE LEAVEN

THE MUSTARD SEED AND THE LEAVEN

S. Matt. xiii. 31-33; *S. Mark* iv. 30-32;
S. Luke xiii. 18-21

I. THE CHARACTERISTICS OF THE KINGDOM

"THE Kingdom of Heaven"—"The Kingdom of God"—what is it? The parables describe its characteristics, its modes of operation and fulfilment. We must try to form some clear conception as to what it meant in the mind of Jesus. The subject demands a treatise—not a paragraph. For its fuller treatment by English writers I can only refer to such books as those of F. D. Maurice, of Dr. A. B. Bruce, of Dr. Stanton, or of the Bishop of Exeter.

For "the Kingdom" the whole experience
of the Old Testament was a preparation;
in "the Kingdom" was summarized the
whole teaching of Jesus; from "the Kingdom" have come all the best and truest
energies of human life; towards "the Kingdom" in its full realization, moves the course
of the world. Our Lord Himself never
gave a definition of His Kingdom; and we
cannot presume to speak where He was
silent. To define a conception so wide and
deep would be to isolate some aspect of it
and thus give to that single aspect an undue
importance. The history of the Christian
religion is full of instances of this danger.
Some, for example, have identified the
Kingdom with the visible, organized
Church; others have declared that it is
exclusively an inward principle. Our Lord
was content to select a phrase striking and
easily remembered, a phrase which gathered
up the spiritual history of His people; to
repeat it, after His manner, over and over
again in different contexts, and thus to leave
it in the minds of His hearers as the centre

of many thoughts and associations. But though it is impossible to define "the Kingdom of Heaven," we may perhaps, without injustice to any of its aspects, describe it as simply the true life—the life which is in free and full accord with the will of God. Our Lord speaks of it in relation sometimes to its inherent qualities of growth and expansion; sometimes to its moral and spiritual characteristics; sometimes to its sources and means of sustenance; sometimes to its outward forms. But in whatever context the phrase occurs it always denotes something vital, energetic, progressive. It is the life which He Himself as "Son of Man" embodied and manifested; the life which, by His words, His example, His spirit, He communicated to His brethren; the life which came from Him by a new birth to the spirit of man, and springing up there flowed out into all the energies of his body and soul; the life with which His Spirit endowed the "body," the community of His Church, and with which that Church should in its turn inspire and transform all

humanity. This is the Kingdom of Heaven
—an inward vital energy moving out from
the King's Spirit, uniting His subjects to
the King's self and to each other in the fellowship of a community, inspiring and en-
abling them to do on earth the King's will.

Is there not need of reviving this conception of the vital, the dynamic character
of the Kingdom of God? Has not our
"Churchmanship," *i.e.,* our membership in
the visible "organ" of the Kingdom, become
something stiff, immobile; a means of satisfying the conscience, rather than of stirring
the will? We profess the faith which the
Church keeps. We attend dutifully the
services which it provides. We even receive
obediently the Sacraments which it dis-
penses. We commend and possibly sub-
scribe to the work which it undertakes. But
are we conscious of the thrill of its life, as we
are of the spring on an April morning? Are
we kindled by the warmth of its spiritual
energy to the flame of sacrifice and service?
I know well that such questions as these
even exaggerated—they suggest the arti-

ficial eloquence of the pulpit rather than any real facts of life. Probably there is not one out of any ten professing "Churchmen" who is accustomed to think of the Church as having a life, a corporate energy, of its own. It is simply an institution. If they think of its life and energy, they think primarily not of spiritual forces which move and act through it, but rather of its "business" as an active institution. In thinking of the family most men know that it has a life of its own, a life of memories, of associations with the living and the dead, of influences subtle and far-reaching, moving, so to say, "in the blood"—a life lying behind and animating the outward activities and characteristics of its members. In thinking of the State, though perhaps less readily, most men know that it too has a great hidden life of its own, a spirit which links the past and the present, an abiding energy which in times of national crisis emerges with surprising force; a set of instincts, of moral and intellectual qualities which determine its place among other States in the

world's history—a life as real though not so
obvious as its immediate political activities.
But, strange to say, in regard to "the
Church," most men have singularly little
effective belief that it is in itself a living
organism, a body in which the Spirit of God
dwells, which possesses, springing from
Him as their source, its own spiritual energies and powers, by means of which "the
Kingdom of God" is ever coming into this
world. Restrained indeed and hindered that
intrinsic spiritual life of the Church is by
the divisions, inconsistencies, worldliness of
its members. But faith in its reality would
surely bring the tokens of its power. The
true "Churchman" is not only one who lives
for his Church, but one in whom his Church
lives, inspiring and animating him with the
energies of the Kingdom of God.

In the parables of the mustard seed and
of the leaven, our Lord describes the way
in which the Kingdom influences men.
They are closely related, but yet distinct.
The former describes the outward signs of
the vital energies of the Kingdom, the latter

the mode of their inward working. Both are alike in this, that they seem primarily to refer to the Church as the visible "organ," through which the Kingdom affects the history and life of the world. The definiteness of the seed and of the leaven, containing yet concealing the inward properties of life and growth, suggests a definite body. Just as physical life, of which we can tell neither the origin nor the destiny, has its organ in the body; just as within the body the faculty of thought which we cannot really explain, finds its organ in the brain; so the Kingdom of Heaven, which is nevertheless wide as the scope of the Spirit of God, finds its special organ in the Church. In these two parables we see the outward sign and the inward process of the life of the Church in the world.

II. THE MUSTARD SEED

"The Kingdom of Heaven is like unto a grain of mustard seed, which a man took

and sowed in his field; which indeed is less
than all seeds: but when it is grown it is
greater than the herbs, and becometh a
tree, so that the birds of the heaven come
and lodge in the branches thereof." (S.
Matt. xiii. 31, 32). "Small as a mustard
seed" was a proverbial expression, common
in popular speech. But with its smallness,
men also noted its qualities of heat, of
strength, and of healing. It may be that
as Jesus spoke He could point to some
mustard tree among whose branches the
birds were sitting. It was an illustration
of the contrast between first beginnings and
final endings, of the powers of growth
which lie hid in first beginnings if only they
are inherently sound and strong.

(1) Surely this parable must have come
back to the minds of the friends of Jesus
with encouragement when, as a small body
of obscure and despised men, they were
bidden to go into all the world and make
disciples of all nations. And to us too who
look back upon the long and chequered
history of the Church, the fulfilment of

its prophetic truth is always encouraging.
Dr. Lightfoot used to say that the study
of history was the best cordial for drooping
spirits. But the study which cheers is that
which takes a wide view over long periods.
When we look round at the position of the
Christian Church in our country to-day,
and note its divisions, its failures, the vast
masses who stand outside it, depression
comes over us. But when we look back
at the position of the Christian Church, say
a hundred years ago, courage returns. We
see in the main real advance; we see signs
everywhere of that astonishing power of
revival of which the Church alone among
human institutions seems to possess the
secret; we are convinced that a power
more than human is necessary to account
for this persistent capacity to survive abuses
so glaring, failures so overwhelming, sloth
so inveterate. The encouragement grows
the further back we cast our glance. It
reaches the point of buoyant faith when,
down the long and confused vista of the
centuries, across the bewildering picture of

the rise and fall of powerful nations and
great ideas, our eyes reach the first century
of the Christian era. Then we realize that
the institution which seems then to be
the very feeblest, the company of fanatical
believers in a crucified Jew, ridiculed and
persecuted, is the only one which has survived the shocks and convulsions of these
nineteen hundred years. The mere survival
of the Church proves that there is that
within it against which "the gates of hell"
cannot prevail—an inherent, indestructible
vitality which comes from the indwelling
Spirit of Him "Who is the Resurrection
and the Life." Thus when the Church
is taunted by its critics to-day with its
divisions, its loss of numbers or worldly
influence, or intellectual strength, its patent
inconsistencies, it will note, and if it can
will remedy, its defects, but it will also
quietly say, "Graviora passi"—"I have
survived greater calamities than these"—
and will fare forth upon its way in faith.

(2) The parable interprets to the Church
not only its general course in history, but

the mode of its successive revivals. They have always, like the mustard tree, grown from small beginnings. The history of the first group in the upper-chamber at Jerusalem has been repeated over and over again; a few devoted men, inspired by the Holy Spirit, have been the seed of great and surprising developments. Think of the little band of monks who landed with Augustine on the shores of Thanet; of S. Columba and his handful of followers who rested their weary oars at Iona; of S. Francis and his first few "poor brothers"; of Charles and John Wesley, with their fellow-students following their "method" of life at Oxford; and remember what great developments grew from such small beginnings. They were known to the Providence of God, but scarcely imagined or imaginable by men when the seed was sown. It is this thought which invests the first faint and apparently fruitless efforts of the missionaries of the Kingdom in distant lands and among strange nations with something more than pathos—with the light of great hope and clear faith. It may almost be said that no great revival or extension of the Christian Church has arisen except from small and even obscure beginnings. The conspicuous and dramatic conversion of Constantine, the baptism, intensely moving as it must have been at the time, of whole nations—these were the seeds not of progress, but of degeneration. Movements which have in them the promise of a great future seldom spring into immediate success. A church discloses the possibility of great things to come, when it is, so to say, in a state of germinating rather than when it is in a state of mere outward success and influence. There is a promise of the future in a church where there are bands of men, however small, who are framing great ideals and making ventures for them, where the old men still dream dreams and the young men are not ashamed to see visions; where new enthusiasms are met not by suspicion but by sympathy, by the wisdom which waits to see whether they be of God. On the other hand a church is surely forfeiting its claim upon the future, however impressive its display of mere power or mechanical unity may be for the moment, when it arrests new movements and stamps them out with iron feet. There is therefore warning as well as encouragement in the parable of the mustard seed. Let us take both to heart.

III. THE LEAVEN

"The Kingdom of Heaven is like unto leaven which a woman took and hid in three measures of meal, till it was all leavened" (S. Matt. xiii. 33). The parable of the mustard seed illustrates the outward signs of the life of the Kingdom; that of the leaven, the method of its inward working. Its influence passes always from within, outward. The leaven contains within itself hidden qualities of expansion and penetration; as soon as it is lodged within the foreign substance, these qualities at once operate, till the whole is leavened. Thus the life of the Kingdom, in the soul or in the world, possesses an inward vitality and energy which at once and with increasing force diffuse their influence.

IV. THE KINGDOM IN THE SOUL

Consider the truth first in its relation to the individual soul. When "the grace of God"—which is nothing else than the infused life of the Christ—is fully and honestly taken into the soul, it quietly and inevitably penetrates and transforms all the capacities and energies of the character. But its law of growth is from within, outward. How often we attempt to reverse the process! In our desires to live rightly, as we say, "to be good," we begin at the circumference of life — business, daily habits, intercourse with others. We make resolutions and frame rules to control this outward life of conduct; and we think that this dutiful, regulated outward life will somehow pass its virtue into the inner soul. Now it is of course right that we should thus bring all our outward life into order; but the rules and resolutions must be the result, the expression, of the inward life. It is the old lesson which S. Paul learned in the bitterness of his own experience and taught once for all in his Epistle to the Romans. The law cannot give life; life must issue in law. To forget this is to entangle ourselves in the struggle and the bondage from which S. Paul was set free. We may go on making rules and breaking them; making them again and striving to keep them better; and yet find that even earnest moral struggle results in little moral progress and brings us no nearer to the sense of freedom. We forget that the *first* thing is by whole-hearted faith and self-surrender to welcome and respond to the grace of God in the inward soul. With all our self-discipline, we must begin, continue and end with "conversion." Then, if at the centre of our life we are really surrendered to God, His grace will work its way out to the farthest circumference of our conduct, permeating as it passes all our desires and thoughts and interests. Learn from the parable of the leaven that first and last lesson of the life of the Kingdom in the soul—that it works from within, outward.

V. THE KINGDOM IN THE WORLD

But it is with the influence of the Kingdom upon the world rather than with its influence upon the soul that this parable is more directly concerned. Yet the law of that influence is the same—it moves from within outwards. It is well for us in these days to remember how wonderfully this law was illustrated in the action of the Church upon the world in the first ages of the Christian era. The leaven was indeed hidden, yet surely and steadily its presence told. Dean Church, in a passage of singular insight and eloquence, has described the process. It is a passage which I at least can never read without deep emotion, and you will forgive me if I quote it at some length. The beginnings of the new morality "were scarcely felt, scarcely known of, in the vast movement of affairs in the greatest of empires. By and by, its presence, strangely austere, strangely gentle, strangely tender, strangely inflexible, began to be noticed. But its work was long only a work of indirect preparation. Those whom it charmed, those whom it oppressed, those whom it tamed, knew not what was being done for the generations which were to follow them. . . . They little thought of what was in store for civil and secular society as they beheld a number of humble men, many of them foreigners, plying their unusual trade of preachers and missionaries, announcing an external Kingdom of righteousness, welcoming the slave and the outcast as a brother, a brother of the Highest, offering hope and change to the degraded sinner, stammering of Christ and redemption to the wild barbarian, worshipping in the catacombs, and meekly burying their dead, often their outraged and murdered

dead, in the sure hope of everlasting peace.
Slowly, obscurely, imperfectly, most imperfectly, these seeds of blessing for society began to ripen, to take shape, to gain power.
The time was still dark and wintry and
tempestuous, and the night was long in going. It is hard even now to discern there
the promise of what our eyes have seen. I
suppose it was impossible then. It rather
seemed as if the world was driving rapidly
to its end, not that it was on the eve of its
most amazing and hopeful transformation."
These words are the best commentary on
the parable. But do they not rebuke many
of our modern methods—impatient of deep
and hidden influence, eager for momentary
success? Does not the Church to-day stand
in danger of reversing the true law of influence—of seeking to work from without in-
wards, of busying itself with the circumference instead of perfecting the centre? Consider the feverish strain or organization,
the eagerness to adopt methods which en-
sure popularity or attract numbers, the
idolatry of indiscriminate energy, which

mark all the efforts of the Church. Consider the want of proportion between the demand for sanitary, industrial, and social reform, and the demand for the deepening and strengthening of the spiritual life. The extension of the true influence of the Church depends upon the intensity of its spirit. Even when most conscious of its call to affect the whole range of national life, to bring within its fold the masses who are straying without, the Church must, by repeated acts of recollection, return to the great saying of its Lord, "For their sakes I sanctify myself." It is by the depth of inward life rather than by the width of outward energy that the Church and its members really and lastingly influence the world.

THE HID TREASURE AND THE
PEARL OF GREAT PRICE

THE HID TREASURE AND THE PEARL OF GREAT PRICE

S. Matt. xiii. 44, 45, 46

I. THE TRUTH POSSESSED

THE two parables of which we have been thinking, describe the progress of the Kingdom of Heaven in the world. The two parables which we are now to consider describe the possession of the Kingdom of Heaven in the individual soul. The coming of the Kingdom is set before us as a personal discovery and acquisition of Truth. But we are still to carry with us our conception of the Kingdom as something vital and energetic. The Truth which is here portrayed as a treasure, as a pearl of great price, is Truth in relationship to life. It is an inspiration and satisfaction of life— an inward energy of faith and power and joy.

This personal possession of the Truth which Christ revealed is fitly described as the "*Kingdom* of Heaven." For it is Truth alone which gives royalty to life. Until we have found and grasped some Truth which we take as giving for us the last word about the meaning of ourselves and of God, our life lacks purpose and consistency. It is swayed about by the events, the impressions, the business, the passions, which encounter us. To them we are subject: it is Truth alone which makes us kings. It gives us the power of choosing our own principles of action, of ordering and arranging our life in accordance with them. In this sense the enthronement of Truth within him makes a man the "master of his destiny." You remember the great words of our Lord in that brief and wonderful colloquy with Pilate. "Thou sayest that I am a King.

To this end was I born, and for this cause came I into the world that I should bear witness unto the Truth." The life of witness to the Truth is the royal life. And for that reason it is the life of freedom. The Truth, said our Lord, shall make you free. We are made for freedom. Man's inborn freedom is the proof of his royal blood— the "image of God" in which he was made. But when it loses hold upon the Truth it becomes self-will, and self-will reveals its error by bringing men under the bondage of sin. It is only when we discover the Truth and make it our own and follow it that we recover our freedom. For the possession of the Truth unites our own will to the free and royal Will of Almighty God. We enter into "the Kingdom of Heaven."

II. THE TRUTH ATTAINED BY SACRIFICE

These two parables are at one in presenting this possession of Truth as

something which demands sacrifice if it is
to be attained. The men sold all that they
had in order to secure their discovery.
When once we have come to take the
Revelation of Jesus Christ as true, there
is only one place which it can fill in our
life—it is the place of supremacy. To
secure it, to realize it as our own, to enjoy
its wealth, we must be ready to make any
sacrifice. We do not possess it if we only
believe that it exists, or that it is of great
value. We do not possess it if we only
discern it—see at times visions of its beauty
and richness, of all that it *might* bring into
our life. We do not possess it even if in
moments of high emotion we seem to feel
and know its wealth and power. Possession is secured only by sacrifice—sacrifice which is willing to cover the whole
range of life. We must be willing to sell
all that we have in order to buy. Is it not
true—do we not in our conscience know it
to be true—that the reason why so many
of us who believe in the truth of our religion, who even have glimpses of its won-

ders and beauty, and occasional experiences of its power, do not really possess it, and are not possessed by it, is simply that we have not yet made up our minds that for us it is to be the supreme thing? It is when we *stake* something for Christ and His Truth, stake some inward struggle or outward service that we begin to make sure of our vital hold upon Him. Certainly those who stake most fully seem always to possess most surely. There are men now working in the native quarter of Calcutta, in the heart of Central Africa, in the crowds of East London, who know that the promise of our Lord is always fulfilled—"There is no man that hath left house or parents or brethren or wife or children for the Kingdom of God's sake who shall not receive manifold more in this present time and in the world to come life everlasting." Your religion will be a possession of happiness and power only in proportion as it is thorough and thoroughness is tested by sacrifice.

III. THE NATURE OF THE SACRIFICE

The nature of the Christian sacrifice
is also explained. It is so sure of the
supreme worth of its object that it is
eager and even joyful. It is expressly
said of the man who found the treasure
that *"in his joy* he goeth and selleth
all that he hath." If a man has really
come to see and know the worth of the
Gospel—that it does bring "salvation,"
that sense of inner *rightness* in relation
to God and self and the world, which
alone can satisfy his life—then the sacri-
fices which he makes to secure it are
lifted and lightened by a certain joyful
ardour. Sacrifice of some sort there must
be in all human life: it arouses either
willing acceptance or grudging submission.
But even the willing sacrifice has two
kinds. It may be that which bends the
head, and shuts the lips, and steels
itself to bear in a proud acknowledgment of the inevitable. It speaks in

the pathetic words of Matthew Arnold,
bidding us

> "Waive all claim to bliss and try to bear;
> With close-lipped patience for our only friend,
> Sad patience too near neighbour to despair."

But there is also the sacrifice which is borne
and even welcomed because it is sustained
by an uplifting trust in the motives of the
Power which asks for it, and in the issue
towards which it tends. It is always true
that "he who saves his life shall lose it":
it is not always true that "he who loses his
life shall save it." For he must know and
trust the ultimate meaning of his loss. Our
Lord's promise is, "He who loses his life
for *My sake and the Gospel's* shall save it."
These additional words take the blindness
and the bitterness out of sacrifice. S.
Augustine found this true in his experience:
"How delightful did it suddenly become to
me to lack all frivolous delights, and those
which I had feared to lose it was now a
joy to forego. For Thou didst cast them
from me who art the true and highest

delight. Thou didst cast them from me
and enter in their place Who art sweeter
than every pleasure." Sometimes, indeed,
the actual pain of the sacrifice is not spared.
Jesus Himself felt it keenly. But the spirit
is sustained by the joy of the issue. It is
said of Jesus that "for the joy that was set
before Him He endured the cross, despis-
ing the shame." Never without struggle
can the Kingdom of Heaven be attained: it
is "the violent" who press into it. To the
outward observer the strain may seem hard
and severe, but he who knows and trusts
what he is seeking will find increasingly
that his faith, his sureness about the worth
of it all, lifts the weight of his burden and
lights the darkness of the way, and brings
even joy into the sacrifice. The spirit
stands erect even when the head is bowed,
and the cross of the Christian, like the cross
of Christ, becomes a throne.

So far the two parables teach a common
lesson. But there is a significant difference
between them, which almost all commen-
tators have noticed. In the first, the treasure

is suddenly and unexpectedly discovered by the labourer as he is at work in the field. In the second, the pearl of great price is the reward of the merchantman's long and eager search. The parables thus illustrate the two chief ways in which the Kingdom of Heaven comes to men. Let us therefore consider very shortly each parable by itself.

IV. THE HID TREASURE

The labourer is working in the field, fulfilling the routine of his daily task. Suddenly his attention is arrested. Perhaps the ploughshare turns over with the earth some unfamiliar object. The labourer stoops down, and he discovers a mass of treasure which some one in these unsettled districts had buried in the soil for safety. So it has often happened in the story of the soul. It may be that while the daily life is running its usual course suddenly some familiar words of the Bible stand out with new clearness, or arrest the conscience with new force

and power. The spirit is seized and stirred
by some new throb of insight or of penitence. I have known, for example, an in-
stance in which the truth and wonder of the
reality of Christ's human nature and sympathy flashed upon a man as he was almost
casually reading a description of the boy-
hood of Jesus. It was hearing the Gospel
for the day in church which changed the
whole life of S. Francis of Assisi. Sometimes a sudden sense of sin and craving for
the assurance of salvation have pressed in
upon the soul with overwhelming urgency.
You remember the life-stories of Bunyan
and John Newton. Some of you may have
been spectators of the strange drama of a
great "revival." Make all allowance for
the atmosphere of a common excitement,
for the mysterious influences of the body
upon the soul; analyze as we will the
"psychology of conversion," and account as
we please for the "sub-conscious self" and
its capacity for sudden emergence into
activity; yet it is impossible to see or hear of
these sudden and surprising movements of

the soul without a renewed conviction that
they are also the signs of that Spirit of God
Who blows where He lists and men cannot
tell whence He comes and whither He goes,
and of the deep and ineradicable correspondence between the need of man and the
Gospel of Christ.

V. THE TREASURE AT OUR FEET

The treasure is hid in the field: it
is not dropped from the skies. What
is new and sudden is not the existence
of the treasure, but the man's discovery of
it. So in the case of these strange illumina-
tions and conversions. However sudden
they may seem, we cannot doubt that all the
while a preparation has been going on in
the soul. The impressions of early experiences apparently forgotten—recollections,
it may be, as Wadsworth thought, of some
higher and purer world—the patient teaching, perhaps in childhood, of parent or
of pastor—old questionings silenced for the

time but haunting still the recesses of the mind—the unconscious influence of the baptismal grace, of the unseen Spirit of God—all these have been "hid in the field" of character and life. How often we learn that some of the most penetrating and enduring influences are those which do their work in silence and in secret. There is the atmosphere of home in early days; there are the prayers and thoughts of those who watch us with silent eyes of love and care both here and surely in the world unseen; there is the quietly diffused power of example, of contact with men and women better than ourselves; above all—how strangely we forget it!—there is the ceaseless working of One Who knows us perfectly and loves even as He knows and who wills that all should be saved and come to the knowledge of the truth. Never let us neglect for ourselves or for others the silent power and steady pressure of education, of atmosphere, of orderly habits, of religion, of the faithful use of appointed "means of grace." The treasure must be prepared and hidden be-

fore it can be discovered. Let us then
neither doubt nor presume upon the liberty
of God's illuminating and converting
power.

VI. THE TREASURE FOUND AND HIDDEN

When the treasure is found, the man
hides it again. Why? In order that he
may thoroughly secure his possession of
it. Not till he has quietly and diligently
sold all he has and bought the whole
field is that security his. Thus when any
sudden illumination or conversion comes,
men are not to suppose that the treasure is
at once and wholly their own. They are
not there and then to drag it forth, to pro-
claim it upon the house-tops, to shout aloud
their discovery of it. They are, on the
contrary, rather to "hide" it—to show their
sense of its tremendous value by a reverent
reserve. Then by diligent self-denial, by
testing their sincerity, they are to buy up
and bring under their control the whole

field of their life and character. Then and
then only can they dare to say that the new-
found treasure is their own. Saul of Tarsus
went from his conversion for three years
into the deserts of Arabia.

VII. THE PEARL OF GREAT PRICE

The Kingdom of Heaven, the possession
of the Truth as it is in Jesus, comes to men
not only as a sudden discovery but also
sometimes as the reward of eager search.
It is the lifework of the merchantman to
find "goodly pearls," and in the course of
his travels he finds one of such supreme
worth that for the sake of it he sells all he
has and buys it. "Goodly pearls" are the
object of the merchant's search. He is a
type of those who view the world as full of
possibilities waiting to be realized, full of
"pearls" of truth and beauty and joy. Life
presents itself to them as a quest, a voyage
of discovery. They are never happy in the
peaceful harbour of routine; they are ever

putting out to sea. Like Tennyson's Ulysses they "cannot rest from travel"; they say, with him,—

"All experience is an arch wherethro'
Gleams that untravelled world, whose margin fades
For ever and for ever when I move."

This is a spirit in itself right and brave and true. He Who made the world and rejoices in it, Who has filled it with such inexhaustible beauty and mystery, Who has endowed us with such powers of feeling and of thought, must surely watch with favour His merchantmen setting out to seek the goodly pearls. It is one of the reasons why we should be thankful for the age in which we live that there is such a stir of travel in the air, such a belief in the wealth which life contains.

VIII. THE QUEST OF THE PEARL

It is a *merchantman* who seeks the pearls, a man whose search is a business demanding and receiving care, thoroughness, concentration. It is the weak and disappointing side of our modern spirit that it is so superficial, so vaguely restless. If we are to find "pearls" we must seek with real deliberation and persistence, not as the *dilettante* but as the merchantman. Dr. Jowett said once, in one of his pithy sermons, "The search for truth is one thing: fluttering after it is another." There is too much of this vague fluttering in the modern spirit. Many people feel the mere seeking, travelling, enquiring so interesting that they are not seriously concerned about the finding. We may be sure that in the spiritual as in the artistic or scientific life, the mere amateur will do no great work and make no great discoveries. You will never get an answer to your questions unless your heart and will are set upon the getting of it.

IX. THE VALUE OF THE PEARL

It has often been pointed out that in the parable the merchant who is seeking goodly pearls finds *one* pearl of great price; and that one pearl satisfies the search for many. He sells all he has and buys it. This goodly pearl of great price is plainly the Truth as it is in Jesus. It is presented to us as a supreme unity—gathering into itself all the truth and beauty which we seek. After all, it is only in some unity—some one truth which sets the place and value of all others —that we can find the satisfaction of the spirit's quest. The man of science, unless he arbitrarily arrests his journey, must pass from the laws whose working he traces, to the nature of the whole of which they are a part. The artist must seek some relationship between beauty and truth and goodness. The philosopher must find the correspondence between truth and life. We all need some point of view from which we can settle the proportion of all the varied elements of our being. It is this single, unifying truth which we believe to be given us in "the Word made Flesh"—in the union of man with God in the person of Jesus Christ. It displaces and thrusts out nothing that the mind of man can truly know or the senses of man can rightly feel. It only brings into one light the scattered rays. It stands apart from the objects of human thought and sensation only because it stands above them and gathers them up into its own unity. It links the universe and all its laws with God, truth with life, beauty with goodness, love with law. But this is a theme too vast and deep for such a paper as this. I cannot do better than close with the words of Dr. Trench: "It is God alone in Whom any intelligent creature can find its centre and true repose; only when man has found *Him* does the great *Eureka* (I have found) burst forth from his lips: in Augustine's beautiful and often quoted words: 'Lord, Thou hast made us *for* Thee, and our heart is restless until it resteth *in* Thee.'"

THE TEN VIRGINS

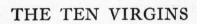

THE TEN VIRGINS

S. Matt. xxv. 1-13

I. THE DIVINE ADVENT

THE parable of the Ten Virgins is one of the most beautiful and yet one of the most searching and solemn of all the parables. Deep as the meanings may be which underlie its details, its main lesson stands out with impressive simplicity, and as we read it experience and conscience are the best interpreters. The setting of the story is the picturesque ceremonial of a Hebrew wedding. When night has fallen, the bridegroom, attended by his friends, proceeds to the home of the bride, claims her, leads her forth with her own maidens to his house or to the place selected for the marriage feast. On the way the procession is joined by other maidens, who are waiting for it, and these all, with lamps or torches in their hands, often with music and singing, pass into the place of banquet. Our Lord speaks, as it were, from the heart of His own people, but the lessons He teaches are for all times. Let us try to learn some of them as we follow the story step by step.

The Ten Virgins go forth to meet the bridegroom and await his coming, as he leads his bride, the prize of his love, with him. We take the Virgins to represent simply our human nature awaiting its true consummation. The universe itself is a traveller, journeying towards the fulfilment of a destiny, yet to be revealed. "For we know that the whole creation groaneth and travaileth in pain together until now." Science calls this strange and toilsome journey "evolution," and can tell us the story of its stages; religion calls it the slowly unfolding Purpose of God. Within this universal movement and expectancy man has his own place—he marches at its head. He is conscious in himself, in body, in mind, and spirit, of his incompleteness, and in that very knowledge he finds the token and pledge of a completeness still awaiting him. However darkened by sin, deluded by mistakes, thwarted by manifold imperfections, he cannot silence that imperious "Forward" which he takes to be the voice of his destiny.

> "Ay, but a man's reach should exceed his grasp.
> Or what's a heaven for?"

Can we at all foreshadow that "Divine event," that completion of man and of the world, that "heaven" in store? To this question science of itself can give no answer: It can speak only of the present and the past. Philosophy essays to answer, and its answer has rich meaning for those who are capable of understanding its modes of thought and speech. But religion gives an answer definite and intelligible to all. It is that the great consummation is the passing, the return, of all things into God, or the union of man, and through man of the world, with God. And the Christian Faith, for vindication of its hope, points back to a Divine Revelation in which the final truth was shown forth. In Christ, the perfect union between the world and man, God was revealed. His spirit is in man and in the world, realizing age by age the union thus revealed. In a word, the great unfolding Purpose of God is, in "the fulness of the times, to sum up all things in Christ." The fulfilment of all that the Incarnation meant is the great consummation. This is, in the language of the New Testament, the coming of the Bridegroom for which the world is waiting.

Again, as in the movement of all things towards the great completion humanity is in the van of the world, so necessarily the Church must be in the van of humanity. For the Church is the "body" in which the Spirit of the Christ dwells, through which as His "organ" (you will remember our thoughts about this in a previous paper) He carries out His great work of gathering all this movement into Himself. The

Church is meant to be—alas! that it should so constantly fail in realizing its true meaning!—that section of humanity which is ever bringing all that is true in life and thought and feeling, "the glory and the honour of the nations," into union with God in Christ. Thus, in the parable the Bride is specially the Church, and the Ten Virgins, the friends of the Bride, are specially the men and women who, as the members of the Church, inspired by its Faith and sustained by its life, are ever working and waiting for the fulfilment of its purpose. The whole meaning of their life is that they have "gone forth to meet the Bridegroom."

Do you complain that these thoughts are too high? that we cannot attain unto them? that they seem indeed not thoughts at all but mere vague high-sounding words? Certainly they represent ways of thinking and speaking very unfamiliar to most of us. But, after all, they are the thoughts and words of the New Testament, especially of S. Paul. They were very rich and inspiring once, in

the great days, for example, of the Church
of Alexandria.   Our modern Christianity
loses enormously in depth and power because our religious perspective is so narrow
and meagre.   Yet it ought not to be difficult
to translate such high themes into the terms
of our experience.   Do we not all know
what it is, in quietly watching some sunset,
to feel a strange yearning, almost a pain of
yearning, for some Beauty which lies beyond? Well, there we had a momentary insight into the incompleteness of a world
which has not yet realized its destiny.   We
felt

> "Those obstinate questionings
>   Of sense and outward things,
>   Falling from us, vanishings;
>   Blank misgivings of a creature
> Moving about in worlds not realized,
> High instincts before which our mortal Nature
> Did tremble like a guilty thing surprised."

But more simply still—do we not all feel
that there is a void in our life, which not
all our interests and cares, all our loves
and friendships can wholly fill?   That the

energies of our being are still desultory and
uncertain, wanting clearness and decisiveness of purpose, that its deepest needs are
still unsatisfied? And, if we are Christians
at all, do we not know that somehow all
this sense of incompleteness, this vague desire, shapes itself more and more distinctly,
into the one single aspiration, "Christ"?
Then, if this be so, we realize what our life
is waiting for: we are likened unto the Ten
Virgins who went forth to meet the Bridegroom.

II. THE LAMP AN OUTWARD SIGN

They "took their lamps." The lamps
were plainly the outward signs that they
were a company awaiting a bridegroom.
This gives us a clue to their meaning in
the parable. If we are companions of the
Bride, Christians, members of the Church,
our "lamps" are the outward signs of our
Christian profession—the religious habits
which we observe, such as prayers, use of
the Sacraments, attendance at Divine

worship, or the good works which because we are Christians we try to do. These are all signs of that attitude of expectancy, that sense of incompleteness apart from Christ, which is involved in the Christian life.

They who say and do such things "declare plainly that they seek a country"—that there is a completion of their life for which they crave. That at least is implied, whether sincerely or insincerely, in the outward signs of Christian profession—in taking our lamps.

III. THE INWARD SPIRIT

The lamp itself cannot shine: the light comes from the oil with which the lamp is filled. "The wise virgins" took the oil with them: the foolish forgot it. In spite of all discussions on the point, there is no real difficulty in interpreting the meaning of the oil. It is that inward spiritual life which alone can give reality and efficacy to the outward life of religion. Both in the Old and the New Testament the symbol of oil is associated with the Holy Spirit. S. John speaks of the Christian having "an anointing from the Holy One." In the ancient hymn of the Church we pray to the Holy Spirit, "Anoint and cheer our soiled face with the abundance of Thy Grace." To have oil in our lamps is to have within and behind all our external acts and habits of religion an interior life of communion with God, in which distractions are removed, the channels between the soul and God are open, so that the Holy Spirit moves through them, fulfilling His work of perfecting the fellowship between man and God. It is to "walk in the Spirit," "to be in the Spirit." Without this oil of the Spirit our lamps have no light. We may be regular and conscientious in our stated prayers, diligent in our attendance at church, in our use of the means of grace. We may be students of the Scriptures, or constant readers of theological books, or experts in theological discussions. We may be intensely interested in Church affairs. We may be "excellent organizers," and full of energy in all sorts of good works. We may be very Marthas in our religious activities. But the one thing needful is lacking—the reality of personal spiritual life, in which, withdrawn from everything external, we are "acquainted with God," and are conscious of a personal relationship, as real and intimate as that which binds us to a friend. There must be the lamp—the outward visible "body" of our religion, the sphere of its witness to the world: but the lamp is useless without the oil—the inner spirit with its own personal hold upon God.

IV. THE TIMES OF SLEEP

"While the Bridegroom tarried they all slumbered and slept. Our Lord speaks here of the inevitable times of reaction, when the first thrill of going forth is past, and for a long spell there are no unmistakable signs of the presence of the Bridegroom. Such times there have been often

in the history of the Church, periods of
pause, when no one seems to have an "open
vision," no prophet speaks as one coming
straight from the Lord before Whom he
stands, no great movement attests the energy
of the Holy Spirit. Perhaps we in this generation have been passing through such a
time of slumber. It is not a time, with all its
merits, conspicuous for high hopes, great
words, striking personalities, or constrain-
ing causes. We feel as if the stream of
Christian life has somehow got locked in a
backwater, and is in danger of becoming
stagnant.

Such periods, again, there must be in
the history of every soul. Probably only
very superficial people or those who are, in
the beautiful Scottish phrase, "far ben," escape this discipline of dullness. But even
then the "wise" man will keep his oil by
him: his soul will still be "waiting upon the
Lord his God." However fruitless it may
seem, he will never give up his times of
quiet prayer and thought. Surely God
marks the pathos of a dumb spirit's plead-

ing. Perhaps when it is least expected a
token of His presence and power will come.

V. THE AWAKENING

At midnight there is a cry, "Behold the
Bridegroom! Come ye forth to meet Him."
Doubtless there is the thought here of the
final coming of the Lord Christ in His
glory.   But it is not surely the exclusive
thought. As Dr. Trench says, "While there
is one crowning advent of the Lord at the
last He comes no less in all the signal
crises of the Church, at each new manifesta-
tion of His Spirit." We spoke just now of
the religious slumber of our own generation. But are there not signs appearing of a
spiritual revival, voices whispering, perhaps, rather than proclaiming, but still
audible, "Behold the Bridegroom!" There
is a growing weariness of religious controversy, a sense of the hollowness of all our
pushing and striving religious organizations, and of the urgent need of a recovery
of the strength and fire of the Spirit. It may

be that this conviction of our need is an advance-messenger of the Lord Himself, summoning us to come forth to meet Him in some new outpouring of His Grace. To the individual soul as well as to the Church there come these heralds announcing the approach of the Bridegroom. Whatever arouses within us some new sense of our need of Christ, it may be the weariness of ineffectual living, or the conviction of some sin brought home to the conscience, or an impatience with our petty inconsistencies and miserable surrenders to evil, or a clear vision of what our life might have of joy and liberty if we only made up our minds to have done with vacillation and wholeheartedly to accept the mastery of Christ: all these are summonses to go forth and meet the Bridegroom. They may be heard also in calls to new and more strenuous acts of service in the cause of God's Kingdom or of His poor. I do not believe that any man with any sort of religious honesty can say that such messengers have never reached him.

VI. THE EXHAUSTED OIL

But these calls when they come are searching tests. "The foolish said unto the wise, 'Give us of your oil, for our lamps are going out.'" Surely these most pathetic words find an echo in many hearts at the present time. The foolish virgins were there in real desire to meet the bridegroom, only at the critical moment when they were asked to go forth the oil which they had allowed to exhaust itself failed them, and they found that their lamps were going out. Our aspirations in this generation are set Christ-wards, but there is little correspondence between them and our honest spiritual grasp or self-discipline. In the day of dullness we have allowed the inner spiritual life to get stale. It has become exhausted, and we have taken no pains to replenish it; and, as Richard Holt Hutton said, "if men come to Christ with exhausted natures they will never know what there is in Him. A generation of which the most impressive characteristic is its spiritual fatigue will never be truly Christian till it can husband its energy better, and consent to forego many petty interests that it may not forego the religion of the Cross." Or, again, there are many men warmly, perhaps enthusiastically, Christian in sentiment, who are vaguely unsettled in their faith, who are ever asking questions and never taking time to answer them, in whose minds the old phrases of the Creed at once arouse a mist of qualifications, evasions, explanations. But a faith so diluted has no spiritual strength: it creates no power of spiritual venture: it is incapable of meeting great calls. When the Bridegroom's coming is announced it can only cry to stronger, simpler natures: "Give us of your oil, for our lamps are going out."

VII. VAIN IS THE HELP OF MAN

"But the wise answered saying, 'Peradventure there will not be enough for us

and you: go ye rather to them that sell and
buy for yourselves.' " A profound and
solemn truth lies hid in these simple words.
The great crises and opportunities of life
can never be met and used by borrowed
spiritual power. Assent to other men's
thoughts can never be a substitute for convictions reached by our own, and in times
of testing, convictions alone can stand the
strain. In the last resort no man can deliver his brother's soul, so that he must let
that alone for ever. We must buy for ourselves, buy the oil of clear faith and spiritual strength from the Spirit of God, and
the price we must pay is our own personal
thought and toil and prayer. While there
is yet time, before the last great chance has
come and gone, let a man be wise and go
and buy. Let him, on his knees alone with
God, face his sins and ask pardon for them,
and set his will against them: let him re-
solve to have done with vacillation and
postponement, and choose his side in the
great contest between faith and uncertainty,
God and the world. Let him in the stress

of his own need lay hold of the power of
God in Christ, even though he wrestle till
the breaking of the day. Then and then
only will he be able to be ready for God's
call, to fulfil his destiny, and "go in with
the Bridegroom to the marriage-feast."

VIII. THE CLOSE OF OPPORTUNITY

"And the door was shut. Afterwards
came also the other virgins, saying, 'Lord,
Lord, open to us.' But he answered and
said, 'Verily, I say unto you, I know you
not.'" The door was shut. There *is,* if
God's great gift of free will be not a delusion there must be, ultimately, the close of
opportunity. Some chance, though we cannot discern it, will be the last. You will
notice that the poor foolish virgins still
keep their first desire: the cry of their
wishes is still "Lord, Lord, open to us." But
there comes a limit to mere wishing—a
time when it is proved finally futile. And
to those who have to the end contented

themselves with sentiments and aspirations
and have postponed decisions and avoided
convictions, the awful word is spoken by
the just and loving judge—"I know you
not." When the close of opportunity has
come He *knows* only those who have set
their minds and souls and wills in prayer
and sacrifice to the life-work of knowing
Him. Surely there is nothing in all Scrip-
ture more solemn, more searching, than this
judgment of mere good wishes. *"Watch,
therefore, for ye know not the day nor the
hour."*

28607

THE TALENTS

THE TALENTS

S. Matt. xxv. 14-30

I. THE STRICT ACCOUNT

THE parables of the Ten Virgins and of the Talents are so closely connected both in the order of S. Matthew's narrative and in their own inner meaning that we must pass at once from the former to the latter. In the last chapter the parable of the Ten Virgins taught us the necessity of keeping the inward spiritual life true and fresh. It was a call to spiritual renewal. Now, we are to learn from the parable of the Talents that a real spiritual life must manifest itself in vigorous and efficient *service*. The true object of "salvation," of inner rightness

with God, is not to save one's own soul, but
to do God service; it is not that we may
be secure, but that God may be glorified.
We are saved in order that we may serve:
and if we refuse the service we may lose
the salvation. Many a spiritual "revival"
has led to disappointment and even shame
because this elementary truth has been
forgotten.

In this parable, as it has been truly said,*
"Christ represents Himself to us under the
figure of what we should call an exacting
man of business of the best type." Such a
figure may at first sight surprise us. But
our ordinary human experience teaches us
that it must be true. Strictness is the truest
kindness. An indulgent master demeans
and spoils his servants. A strict master
honours and raises them by entrusting even
the meanest with a definite responsibility,
and expecting him to fulfil it. So God's
justice is part of His love. Because He
loves He trusts: He invests His servants

* Bishop Gore's "Charge to the Diocese of
Worcester," p. 1.

with the honour of responsibility; and because He trusts, His claims are high and His demands exacting. His love gives responsibility; His justice demands efficiency of service. We dishonour God if we think of His love as a mere tolerant good nature; God would dishonour us if He accepted indifferent and casual service.

The central figure in the parable is the timorous and diffident servant. Our Lord often surprises us by selecting for special warning those whom the world would be ready to excuse or even to admire. Here we would expect Him to select one of those to whom great opportunities were given as His example of the abuse of trust. As for this obscure servant, with his one poor talent—he is respectable, he is honest, he is neither wasteful nor fraudulent; he is only distrustful of himself, diffident, and unambitious. Surely he might be excused. But no: it is just he who is sent into "the outer darkness." His very diffidence is turned against him—if he was not largeminded enough to understand his Master's purpose, or brave-spirited enough to make ventures in His cause, at least his very fear might have impelled him to be active. "Thou wicked and slothful servant, thou knewest that I reap where I sowed not, and gather where I did not scatter: thou ought-est therefore to have put my money to the bankers, and at my coming I should have received back mine own with interest." It is true that God's claim is always in propor-tion to the opportunity He gives: that to whom little is given of him little shall be required. But the lesson of the parable is that that little shall be required exactly and with interest. Are there not thousands of quiet, respectable men and women, who shelter themselves behind the obscurity of their lives and the smallness of their endow-ments, and never venture forth under the pressure of a great ideal, and contentedly believe that God cannot expect open and strenuous service from them? It would never occur to them that they of all people were in special danger of the doom of the outer darkness.

II. THE USE OF NATURAL GIFTS

Consider our use of natural gifts or endowments. It is by a true instinct of interpretation that our common English speech has borrowed from this parable the word "talents." The phrase is itself a good sermon. It teaches us that these natural endowments are given to us by our Maker and Master on trust that we shall improve them; educate them, put them out to trade; and this, not for our own sake only, but for His glory. It is this thought which gives to all true education a religious value and sanction. To educate ourselves is part of the duty which we owe to God, and any education in which men wilfully stop short of the best, the fullest possible, is not religious education. Religious education is not merely instruction in religion; it is the utmost development of our faculties of which we are capable for the glory of God. Life is, therefore, one long continuation school, and every true servant of God must be one of its scholars. I may most confidently say that no one who reads these pages is without some natural gift or capacity, however humble, some special taste or aptitude of mind or body. If it be only one, it is a talent with which we are to trade that it may be increased. Christian people have special need of the reminder that the development of natural talent is an integral part of Christian service. The Christian mind has dwelt—I do not say too earnestly, for that would be impossible, but—too exclusively on salvation from the sin by which human nature has been ruined, too little on consecration of the gifts with which human nature has been endowed. But even on the cross of Christ human life was not so much crucified as made capable of consecration. Christ came that we might have life, and have it more abundantly. It is worth while to think that among the questions of the great day of account not the least disquieting to religious people may be those which ask what they have done with the natural talents committed to their charge.

III. THE USE OF SPIRITUAL
ENDOWMENTS

Consider, also, our use of spiritual endowments. Here, again, we cannot honestly plead that we have none. The very instinct of religion is itself one—one which raises the humblest man to a point in the scale of creation immeasurably higher than the noblest animal. It is this instinct of religion which we are asked to strengthen and deepen by care and thought and effort. Is it not true that the average Englishman is sensible of the need of hard work in every other sphere of life except religion? Elsewhere he is strenuous and active: there he is curiously indolent. He seems to think that religion requires nothing more for its sustenance than occasional feelings or a few acts of dutiful observance. It is true, of course, that its source is the Spirit of God, but in this, as in all His gifts, the Spirit of God requires the co-operation of the spirit of man. It is true that we are

inheritors of the Kingdom of God, but it is
only by the output of thought and will that
we can realize our heritage. Let us apply
this truth to two necessary parts of religion
—study and prayer.

Study. How many of us can say at
this moment that we are engaged in some
definite study of a book of the Bible or of
Christian doctrine? Are we not apt to take
some limited point of Christian truth—the
tradition in which we were brought up, the
presentment of Christian doctrine to which
we are accustomed, it may be the truth
which first appealed to us—and "bury it in
the earth," keeping jealous guard over it,
almost suspecting any addition to it! But
there is no Christian truth, however simple,
which would not, if only we thought it out
and "traded" with it, lead us by its own
kinship with them to other truths, wider,
deeper, and higher. We must "follow on,"
by thought and study, "to know the Lord."
Otherwise we stand in danger of losing even
the talent which we had—and what was
once a truth becomes, often without our

knowing it, a form. "For unto every one that hath shall be given; but from him that hath not even that which he hath shall be taken away."

Prayer. No one, surely, can deny that he has the instinct of prayer. Even among the least religious it proves itself to be, in times of anxiety or sorrow, almost invincible. In its simplest form it is a gift most wonderful—a token of the kinship which, deep-set in the very elements of being, binds the children to the Father. Yet how little trouble we take to improve our power of prayer, how feeble are the ventures of faith or perseverence which we throw into it! We know the excuses which are ready upon our lips: "I find my prayers so difficult, so unreal. I have no power of imagination, or thought, or expression. If God expects from me eager and fervent prayers, He is expecting to reap what He has not sowed, and to gather what He has not scattered." It is the very plea of the slothful servant; and, like him, we are content merely to keep the talent, to be satisfied with some

routine of prayer as a duty for the day.
But are we to expect that we can compass
a thing so wonderful as converse with God
without patient and persevering effort? Let
us lay the truth to heart, that what God
values, in prayer, what He most certainly
rewards, is not the immediate fervour of
feeling, but the loyal setting of the will
towards Himself. We are often nearest
God when we *feel* Him least. For prayer
which perseveres in spite of dryness of
feeling is for that very reason a real venture
of faith. As such it earns its interest, the
interest of added strength of will, clearness
of purpose, peace of conscience. The mere
act of prayer, if only a sincere will is behind
it, is as it were a hand stretched out in the
darkness to God. His hand will meet it
even if we do not feel the grasp. To one
who was in trouble because of the want of
any felt satisfaction in prayer, a wise man
said: "If you have not gained a sense of
the presence of God, you have gained the
next best thing, a sense of His absence."
To realize the desire for God, is to have

that hunger of the soul which He is pledged to satisfy, and this of itself lifts a man far above the mass who neither know the joy of God's presence, nor feel the pain of His absence.

IV. THE USE OF OPPORTUNITIES OF SERVICE

Consider finally, and chiefly, the use of our opportunities for active service in the Kingdom of God. There is no question that by our baptism our life stands under the pledge of service. It is not the privilege of the few, but the duty of all. The living Christ is ever in the van of all efforts to rescue and redeem the world, and every Christian must be there at His side. He cannot be "in Christ" sharing his victory without being "with Christ" sharing the toil of His service. No man can be in the true sense a Christian who does not know and keep some definite place in the labours of Christ's Kingdom. For some talent, some opportunity of influence, some chance of work we all possess. God never set any man in any part of His universe without setting some opportunity of service at his side. Whatever it may be, we are to begin there and work in a great spirit.

What is wanting is not the work, but the vigilance to see it, the readiness to welcome it, the eagerness to do it. Men are so apt to plead—"I am so unimportant; my gifts are so few; I am beset by temptations; I find it hard enough to keep my own life straight." But such excuses only echo the plea of the slothful servant; and they lead to the outer darkness. Or, when we have undertaken some work, we are so easily depressed and discomfited. "The difficulties are too great; the failures are manifest; there seems to be no result; it is not worth while to go on struggling with the impossible for ever!" Thus, we lose hope and energy and vigilance for new chances, and readiness for new ventures, and sink back into some mere routine of duty, where at least we are within the region of the possible. But in God's sight the worth of our life is never the success which it secures, but always the spirit which it puts forth. We are better men if we fail in a high endeavour than if we succeed in a meagre one. The great thing is to be up and doing, to be strengthening the world's hard upward course, and resisting its easy downward course, by the resolute output of faith and effort.

There are many signs that we have come to a time in the history of God's Kingdom when it is just the acts of quiet, individual, personal service which are specially needed. We have too long entrusted the work of the Kingdom to particular classes, such as the clergy, to schemes and societies, and all sorts of public organizations. The comparative failure of these public and official efforts must compel us to summon a power higher and stronger than any which they possess—the power of personal influence. Never was charity so widespread and enthusiastic, but alas! at least in our great cities, it has done almost as much to degrade as it has done to raise the poor. And why? Because it has neglected the one really strong power of uplifting—personal care and thought and persistence. We are anxious, in the midst of endless controversies, as to the future of religious education in our schools. Is not this very anxiety meant to send us back to God's own appointed school, the home, and to His own appointed teachers, the parents, that we may make both efficient?

Here then it is—in this region of small things and personal efforts, of single talents, that we are to make our ventures of faith. There is no truth more wonderfully borne out by experience than that the one talent when put out to trade in a spirit of faith and prayer grows in value. Almost all the great movements which have revived religion and relieved the poverty and suffering of this world have arisen, as the parable of the mustard-seed taught us, from small beginnings used in a courageous and faithful spirit. To come to a humbler level, could any opportunity of service seem less

than that of a poor mechanic, condemned
for long years to his bed by a distressing and
incurable illness? Yet I have known such
a man make his sick-room the centre of a
remarkable and widespread spiritual influence among all classes of men, and collect
in a single year, while he himself for his
own wants depended partly on poor relief,
more than one hundred pounds for the
work of Christ's Church. These surely are
the servants whom the King delights to
honour. There are two surprises—one may
venture to think—which await us in the day
when the Lord returns to make His reckon-
ing with His servants. One, the place of
honour given to plain, simple men and
women, who put a great spirit of service
into humble opportunities; the other, the
open and tragic shame of multitudes of
feeble, self-centred, respectable people,
who buried their talents in dull and com-
placent routine. In the spiritual world, the
path of ease and safety is the path of peril[1];
for, in the noble words of Samuel Rutherford, "the safest way, I am persuaded, is to

tyne* and win with Christ, and to hazard fairly for Him; for heaven is but a company of noble venturers for Christ."

V. THE LABOUR NOT IN VAIN

If—but only if—we are thus trading zealously and eagerly with our talents, "hazarding fairly for Christ," then even we can venture sometimes to look forward to the great words of the Lord of Life, words in which life on this scene finds its crown and consummation, words whose very sound is music in the march of duty—"Well done, good and faithful servant: enter thou into the joy of thy Lord." Even here, as bodily exercise sends a glow of health and delight into all the limbs, so resolute and brave-hearted service brings into the very midst of toil and stress a deep sense of joy —the joy of one who knows that what he does is infinitely worth doing.

* That is, *lose*.

If there is any worker in the world who can sing a song of courage it is the fellow-worker with Christ; for he, above all men, knows that "his labour is not in vain in the Lord." Yet, after all, these moments of joy are but foretastes of that which is to come—rather, airs cheering and inspiriting, reaching us in the plain from the high lands where the joy of God is the abiding atmosphere. When the time comes, it is into that joy of his Lord that the faithful servant is ushered, the joy of "heaven," of the life where God's will is eternally done, His purpose eternally fulfilled, His rest eternally assured. As Leighton beautifully said:* "It is but little we can receive here, some drops of joy that enter into *us;* but there *we* shall enter into joy, as vessels put into a sea of happiness." It is a thought which we can only dare to frame for ourselves in the pauses of resolute and unceasing service; but when it rises before us, the thrill of expectancy which it arouses sends

* Quoted by Trench, p. 278.

into all the labour a spirit at once of ardour and of peace. The other day I received a letter from a stalwart labourer in dockyard and church, whose terse words I would pass on to my readers as a summary of all that makes work worth doing and toil worth bearing—"Cheer up, dear sir, there is rest ahead: we shall soon hear the 'Come up' and the 'Well done.'"

THE GOOD SAMARITAN

THE GOOD SAMARITAN

S. Luke x. 30-37

I. WHO IS MY NEIGHBOUR?

THE story of the good Samaritan is one of our Lord's greatest and most typical parables. It is so simple that a child can read its meaning; yet it is in truth a treatise on practical ethics more profound in thought and more powerful in effect than any other in the world. Is it too much to say that in these few verses there is contained the essential truth of man's relations with his fellow men? Our very familiarity with the parable blinds us to the greatness of its mingled simplicity and depth and— let us add—to the greatness of the claim which it makes upon us. We can only gather one or two lessons from its store.

Consider the deep principle of human conduct—we might almost call it the philosophy of life—which the parable contains. We discover the clue to it when we notice that the parable does *not* answer the lawyer's question. The question was: "Who is my neighbour?" The parable tells what it is to be neighbourly. It seems to be a case of logical *non sequitur*. In fact, it is a case of the truth which is deeper than logic. Our Lord could not teach the truth by answering the question. For the question itself was wrong; it revealed a wrong temperament of mind. It was facing not truth but the fundamental error; to follow it therefore would have been to lose the truth. The lawyer, steeped in all the traditions and instincts of his class, wanted our Lord to give him a clear and precise definition of his neighbour; to mark him out, and set him apart from the general mass of mankind. But definition means limitation. If our Lord had said, "*This* man is your neighbour," the inference in the lawyer's mind would have been, "Then that other is *not* my neighbour; I need not concern myself with him; I can pass him by." But this conclusion would have been the very error which Jesus came to banish. He could only put the man right by declining to answer the question; by taking him to a wholly different standpoint, and making him start there, namely—"Be in your own spirit neighbourly, and then every man will be your neighbour."

It is worth while to pause here to notice the light which our Lord's method of dealing with the question of the lawyer throws on what may often be our Lord's method of dealing with the questions which we ask now. In our religious and moral difficulties we throw out some question as a sort of challenge, persuading ourselves that it is really decisive. Often it remains unanswered. We are disappointed, discomfited. Under such failure of their self-chosen test questions, men often give up their faith or surrender their moral struggle. But, apart

from the petulance, the impetuosity, or the
effort to "justify oneself" which a little
honest self-scrutiny would often discover
in our questions, and which are sufficient to
deprive them of any right to an answer—
God's wisdom may see that they spring
from a wrong attitude of mind, that they
are not facing the line of truth, and therefore refuse to answer them. But all the
while in some other way, at the moment
perhaps not discerned, He may be leading
us to the truth. While our mind remains
a blank as to that particular difficulty which
we thought of such crucial importance, He
may be bringing some other truth before
us, or shaping our lives by some special experience, so that after a time we shall find,
perhaps without knowing how, that that old
question has been answered in some other
way, or has been proved futile or superflu-
ous. Often when we have been discussing
their difficulties with some impetuous boy
or some eager but ignorant workingman,
we have realized how hopeless it would be
to answer their clamant questions without

correcting their assumptions or returning to first principles. It would be well for ourselves to see here an analogy with the light in which our own impatient questions must be viewed by the patient wisdom of God and a reason why they so often seem to go unanswered.

II. THE SPIRIT OF NEIGHBOURLINESS

In order to know who is our neighbour we must first possess the true spirit of neighbourliness. It is the spirit of love which knows no limitations. The natural man always tends to look at his relationship with his fellows in the light of the lawyer's question: to regard as his "neighbours"—as men who have a claim upon his thought and help—persons clearly defined and set apart by distinctions of race, class, occupations, locality, and the like. The Jew, in spite of the generosity towards the stranger of his own Law, would regard his fellow-Jew as a neighbour; but he had "no dealings with the Samaritan." The whole system of caste is an elaborate definition and restriction of the neighbour. The spirit of the East is wonderfully described in Arnold's poem, "The Sick King at Bockhara," in which the Vizier taunts the king with his foolish compassion—

> "The Kaffirs also, whom God curse,
>   Vex one another night and day.
> There are the lepers and all sick;
>   There are the poor who faint alway.
> All these have sorrow and keep still
>   While other men make cheer and sing.
> Wilt thou have pity on all these?
>   No: nor on this dead dog, O King."

The free citizen of Greece or Rome saw no neighbour's claim in the subject or the slave. Even now, the white man's civilization when it is left to itself regards the coloured man as a chattel for its own convenience, not as a neighbour entitled to its care and compassion. Dr. Trench quotes a striking passage from the Essays of Emerson—in many ways a type of "the natural man" at his best—"Do not tell me, as a good man did to-day, of my obligation to put all poor men into good situations. Are they *my* poor? I tell thee, thou foolish philanthropist, that I grudge the dollar, the dime, the cent, given to such men as do not belong to me, and to whom I do not belong." We are always inclined to treat as our neighbours only those who can come within the narrow circle of our own duties, or tastes, or sentiments. The remedy lies not in enlarging these circles or adding to our lists so much as in changing our whole point of view. We are to have—so to say—a soul of neighbourliness for man as man.

It was this revolution in man's way of looking at his fellows which Jesus came to accomplish. If we may dare to put it thus boldly—God made Humanity His neighbour. Beholding Humanity robbed of its true nature, stripped of its ideal, wounded by its sins, unable to rise, He came down to it, entered it, healed, and restored it. He "was made man." The Incarnation has made human nature itself sacred. The

Christian, the follower of Christ, must therefore see in every man his neighbour. The claim is not his class or condition, but his mere humanity. And the Incarnation not only revealed this ideal of neighbourliness, but made it possible for us to realize it. Man in himself we might not be able to love—but the Christ in man we can. "St. Francis," we are told, "was riding one day near Assisi while he was still perplexed as to the nature of his future work, when suddenly he was startled by a loathsome spectacle. A leper was seated at the roadside. For a moment he gave way to natural horror, till he remembered that he wished to be Christ's soldier. Then he returned and dismounted and went up to the poor sufferer and giving an alms kissed lovingly the hand which received it. Strong in his hard-won victory he rode on; but when he looked back, there was no beggar to be seen; and therefore his heart was filled with unutterable joy, for he knew that he had seen the Lord." So in his simple way he realized the truth of neighbourliness which he afterwards taught his brothers. "When thou seest a poor man, my brother, an image of Christ is set before thee. And in the weak behold the weakness which He took upon him."

III. PRIEST AND SAMARITAN

Turn next to the parable itself—the application of the general truth. It was a Samaritan who "proved himself neighbour"; the priest and the Levite failed in the test—they "passed by on the other side." Our Lord thus gives a revelation of real, and a rebuke of unreal, religion. The Priest and the Levite represent formal, organized religion; the Samaritan represents the essential spirit of religion. Let us not make the common and foolish mistake of supposing that Jesus meant to condemn the religion of the Priest and Levite, and to commend the religion of the Samaritan. He himself loyally conformed to the religion of the Hebrews: He con-

fessed that the way of salvation was with
the Jews. He chose the Samaritan in the
parable simply in order to strengthen His
rebuke of the Priest and Levite. It was
left to a Samaritan to show the Priest and
the Levite how miserably they had failed to
hold the spirit of true religion with its
form. Let us try to apply the rebuke to our
own times. Alas! it is sorely needed.

The Christian Church exists in the world
to be the organized embodiment of the
Spirit of Christ. When it has been true to
itself, it has been faithful to this high office.
It was the early Church which made the
world see what the Spirit of Christ was, by
its instinctive and eager compassion for the
poor, the slave, the diseased, the afflicted.
At its best, to use the noble words of Dr.
Liddon, the Church "everywhere stands
before humanity not as a patroness but as
might be a loving and faithful servant, who
is too loyal, too enamoured of her master's
name and birthright to be otherwise than
affectionate and respectful in the hour of
his poverty and his shame." However nat-

ural it may be for "the world" to keep sorrow, suffering, poverty, out of its sight, as things which disturb its enjoyment of life or provoke its inconvenient conscience, to "pass them by on the other side," the Christian Church must, so far from avoiding, seek them out and cheerfully accept them as opportunities for service. It must always be on the side where need and distress are lying. This ought to be the very instinct of its life.

But there are times when the Church forgets its primary duty. Wealth, comfort, ease, enfeeble the energy of its compassion. The smoothness of conventional routine deadens its spirit. Or, it becomes overoccupied with its interests and claims as an institution, with the elaboration of its ceremonies, with controversy about its doctrines, and its character as a brotherhood of service grows faint and feeble. It becomes the Priest and the Levite and passes by on the other side. Then it is that the Samaritan is sent to rebuke it and recall it to its true life. The Spirit of the Divine Neigh-

bour, finding Himself straitened and
thwarted in His own Body, turns to those
who are without, and finding a welcome
there, inspires them to do the service which
the Church leaves undone.

Are there not signs at the present time of
such a situation? The Bishop of Southwark recently expressed these signs as a
weakening of "embodied" and a strengthening of "diffusive" Christianity. He
meant that whereas the Church as an
organized institution seems to make less
way than at other epochs, there is, outside
its borders or at least in no formal connection with it, a singular activity of the Christian spirit of sympathy and brotherliness.
The fact is partly an encouragement; it
proves the width and freedom of the Spirit
of Christ in man, that far beyond the limits
of His Church, He is ever active in the
spirit of man, ennobling and inspiring it.
But the fact is also a rebuke to the Christian Church. If it were true to itself, surely
it would attract and enlist in its service and
not repel all this diffused Christian spirit.

It is bound, for the sake of man, to guard the historic Faith. In an age of materialism, it is justified in making its worship a witness to the dignity and mystery of the things unseen and eternal. But does it, with anything like equal zest, keep its heart of service strong and ardent? Does it seem natural to us to describe a body, divided into rival sects and filling the air with the discordant cries of controversy as a brotherhood of neighbourly service? I am not thinking of the noble efforts of individuals and groups within the Church, but of the Christian body as a whole. Does it present itself to men as a Community in which each member, because he is a member, is actively engaged in the service of the weak, the poor, the distressed? On the other hand, we see men and women, weary of Church-wrangles, standing outside the pale even of the Christian Faith, spending and spent in the service of their fellows; and we realize that still it is often the Priest and the Levite who pass by on the other side, and the Samaritan who crosses over and tends and

serves and "proves himself neighbour."
There is surely no ambition which ought to
be nearer the heart of every Christian than
that by his influence and example he may
make the Christian community a worthier
reflection of the Divine Neighbour, who is
ever in the midst of men "as one that serves."

IV. UNSELFISH SERVICE

Consider also the character of the service
which the true neighbour renders. It is un-
selfish, thorough and personal. It is unself-
ish. There is a compassion which is selfish;
and it is very common. Its motive sometimes is the indulgence of sentiment. The
sentiment of compassion like other natural
emotions craves satisfaction. It is really
selfish when its primary motive is to satisfy
itself rather than the need of its recipient.
The charity which relieves itself by giving
an alms to any beggar who asks without
thought or care for his real need, which
does not consider that that alms may be a

means of encouraging thriftlessness and imposture, may be thus a cruel wrong both to the beggar himslf and to the really deserving poor; the charity which, moved by some sentimental appeal, takes no trouble to see whether that appeal is true to facts, or likely to do more harm than good—this charity is fundamentally false; it is a form of self-indulgence. Or, again, the motive may be one's own spiritual good. To give an alms as a means of relieving one's conscience, or acquiring credit in the eyes of God, is really a selfish act. It is not admirable, it is merely pitiable, to see the crowds of beggars at some church door in Italy, maintained in beggary rather than lifted out of it, encouraged to trade in the apparatus of misery, by the alms of the faithful. True charity, true neighbourliness, considers first not the indulgence of sentiment or the satisfaction of conscience, but the true need of the poor. And it has come to pass, through the abuse of charity, that the true need of the poor is often best served by withholding, not giving, the heedless and casual dole.

V. THOROUGH SERVICE

The service of the Good Samaritan is thorough. He discerns and meets all the requirements of the case. He binds up the wounds, he pours in oil and wine, he carries to an inn, he provides for the future. He aims at the entire restoration of the poor stranger. Thus true charity is not content till it has thought out the real need of each case, and the best means of meeting it so as to prevent its recurrence. That thinking out is not easy; it demands time and trouble. In the complexity of social life, each single case of poverty or need is a problem demanding the exercise of the best judgment. If we undertake to meet it we are bound, for its own sake, to give it thought and care, and if we cannot do this, to entrust it to those who can. The parable of the Good Samaritan, so far from encouraging, in truth rebukes haphazard, heedless, indiscriminating charity.

VI. PERSONAL SERVICE

The service which the Samaritan rendered was personal. He himself bound up the wounds, himself set the stranger on his own beast, himself brought him to the inn and took care of him. Charity is always incomplete unless it involves this element of personal service. In these days, we have become too much accustomed to acting the neighbour by deputy. We give money; we leave it to others to give personal service. Of course, to a large extent this is a necessity of modern life; and we can keep even this second-hand charity at least in touch with true principles if we take pains to follow our money with personal interest and sympathy. But we must never be satisfied with this. No amount of subscriptions can compensate for this want of the touch of person with person; of heart reaching heart; of will encouraging and strengthening will. Each one of us ought to be able to think at once of some individual or family in the ranks of the poor, the sick, the distressed, whom by personal thought and care and act we are trying to comfort and cheer and raise. We shall never realize our fellowship with the Divine Neighbour of humanity unless our own mind and heart and will are going out in personal service to some of those who need and claim our compassion.

THE BARREN FIG-TREE

THE BARREN FIG-TREE

S. Luke xiii. 6-9

I. THE DIVINE DISAPPOINTMENT

THIS is a parable easy to understand—taken from Nature, that great open Book of Parables which "he who runs may read." In the corner of the vineyard, protected by its walls, and nourished by its specially prepared soil, a fig-tree has been planted. For two years the lord of the vineyard has come eagerly expecting to see the promised fruit. For two years he has suffered disappointment. On the third year his patience is at an end. The tree is a failure. It is exhausting the soil and hindering the other plants and his sentence goes forth: "Cut it down; why cumbereth it the ground?"

But identifying himself with the tree in the friendly sympathy for his plants which is one of the marks of gardeners— that most attractive class of men—the vine-dresser pleads for it; that for one year more he may be allowed to dig around its roots and fill the spaces with manure, and give it thus another trial.   And the parable ends leaving the fig-tree with a great hope over it, "if it bear fruit, well"; but also a great risk; "if not, then after that thou shall cut it down."

Primarily, doubtless, the parable applies to the Divine disappointment caused by the religious barrenness of the Jews, in spite of God's choice of them and of all the care which He had lavished upon them. To them were given the adoption and the glory and the covenants, and the giving of the law, and the service of God, and the promises."   Yet there was no fruit with which God could be pleased in the dry and lifeless religion of scribe and Pharisee. But the parable has also its lesson for every age. Let us try to learn it.

Our life also has been planted in a vineyard chosen and guarded by God's fatherly care, in a soil of special richness. We have been born in a Christian country, inheriting the traditions of centuries of Christian life, protected by centuries of Christian custom. By baptism, we were planted in that Body in which all the life-giving energies of the Divine Spirit are ever ready for our growth and nurture. There we were made "members of Christ, children of God, and inheritors of the Kingdom of Heaven." Every gift that was needed for our Godward growth was bestowed upon us. Yet when we look at our lives as they really are, can we say that they show signs of growth corresponding to all these possibilities with which we were endowed? Let memory take its stand at any point in our past life, and review the years which have since passed. Are we nearer to God in thought and plan and purpose? Has it become more natural to us to spend a large part of our time in communion with God? And yet, why should it not have been so? Why should there not be a constant and increasing vitality of the spirit corresponding to all this rich endowment which is bestowed upon us? What examples there are stored for us in the memory of the Church! What inspiration lies in the words of the Creed which we continually repeat! And yet, how listless, inert, and dull our Christian life at the best seems to be. I often think of the words of an earnest agnostic. He said: "If I could believe one-tenth part of what you Christians profess, I think there is nothing I could not venture and suffer, and yet, when I go to your churches, how dull and tame and heavy you Christians seem!"

When we think of the great acts of worship and communion in which we engage, do we not feel that we are often like listless actors repeating their lines and performing their prescribed motions? That is the original force of the word "hypocrite." Surely there is scarcely any prayer which we Christians ought to have more constantly in our hearts than this: "From all hypocrisy, good Lord deliver us." And if we, at our best moments, feel, as we must feel, this heart-sickness at ourselves—how can we measure the disappointment of the God Who made us? Was it for these poor, puny, trifling lives, with their little concerns of money and pleasure, their ignoble aims and petty sins, that God Almighty gave us our birth in nature and our new birth in Christ?

II. CONVENTIONAL CHRISTIANITY

But notice again, the barren fig-tree cumbers the ground. This lifeless, unprogressive, conventional Christianity into which we are all so apt to slip, it also cumbers the ground. To give the force of the word in the parable, it does mischief to the ground; it is a waste of grace, a restraint upon the Spirit of God. It checks the enthusiasm of others, it tempts men to doubt whether there is any reality in our religion at all. Can we exaggerate the effect of the inconsistencies of Christians upon the minds of honest men, who are standing critical and suspicious without? Certainly we can never measure the damage which Christianity suffers in the eyes of the heathen when they take the average Englishman abroad as the type of his religion. But let us remember that just in proportion as we allow our Christian life to become dim, our will feeble, and our spirit listless, so we are contributing to this mass, this dead-weight, of staleness which lies so heavy upon the Christian Church, and buries the tokens of the living Christ through Whose presence it was meant to arise and shine. Truly, shall we exaggerate if we say that if God were merely just when He came and visited our life, He would say, "Cut it down; why cumbereth it the ground?"

III. THE PLEADING OF CHRIST

Why is it that God is so patient? It is because the Vine-dresser is pleading for the the barren fig-tree. The Son of Man, to Whom this poor, unworthy humanity has been committed, has identified Himself with the plants of the vineyard. He has covered them, as it were, with His own perfect obedience and correspondence to the Will of God. He has obtained the right to plead that they should be spared yet awhile, and any honest confession of our barrenness brings us within the protection of that prevailing plea.

But we cannot, we dare not, presume upon that protection; we cannot ask the Vine-dresser to plead for us that we may yet be spared; unless we remember the very conditions of his plea—that he may be allowed to take the tree in hand and work His will upon it. Then, and only then, if it bears fruit, well—but if not, it must be cut down. Our penitence must become sur-

render to His will that He may discipline
and re-create us. It is only through growing and bearing fruit that we can attain
the "assurance of salvation."   He Whom
we plead as an Atonement for us must be
accepted as the Master-spirit within us.
Only through daily submission to His influence can we begin at last to bear fruit and
stand the scrutiny of God.

IV. ABIDING IN CHRIST

Our Lord Himself has put the truth in
the plainest words: "He that abideth in Me
and I in him, the same bringeth forth much
fruit; for apart from Me ye can do nothing.
If a man abide not in Me, he is cast forth
as a branch and is withered, and men gather
them and cast them into the fire, and they
are burnt."

What then, is this "abiding in Christ"?
It is the daily merging of our life in all its
purposes, desires, and plans in His.   So

described, it seems very far from any attainment of ours. But let me point to at least four simple means by which a man can in some degree make sure of "abiding in Christ."

The first is Faith—the deliberate converging of all the capacities of our life upon one supreme fact—Christ the Way, the Truth, and the Life. As faith looks at life, it sees one great purpose standing over it—Christ's Will; one great Presence consecrating it—Christ's Spirit.

Secondly, Prayer. Prayer is the inward activity of faith. It means the uplifting of our souls in desire, affection, and will to God as the supreme end of our life. If our prayers are to be the means whereby we secure our abiding in Christ, their main object must be not to get what we want, but to give what God wants—a life surrendered to Himself. Such prayer is the best test as to whether our life is or is not abiding in Christ. If you wish for a simple principle by which you can know whether any pursuit, or ambition, or course of conduct, or friendship is really true to the spirit of Christ, think only whether you can ask Him to accept and bless it in your prayers. William Law has put this test in his usual trenchant way. "Let us suppose," he says, "that a rich man was to put up such a prayer as this to God: 'O Lord, I Thy sinful creature, who am born again to a lively hope of glory in Jesus Christ, beg of Thee to grant me a thousand times more riches than I need; grant that as the little span of life wears out, I may still abound more and more in wealth, and that I may use and perceive all the best and surest chances of growing richer than any of my neighbours. This I humbly and fervently beg in the Name of Jesus Christ, Amen.'" An impossible prayer, but, alas! a life too possible and too frequent. We may depend upon it that "the same things that make an unchristian prayer, make an unchristian life." On the other hand, any desire or action of our life which will really stand the test of honest prayer, we may humbly take as "abiding in Christ."

Thirdly, Self-discipline. It is plain that if we are to keep our life in union with Christ, self-discipline is all essential. The road in which Christ's companionship is assured is the road of the daily cross. The Cross must come to us, not only in power to forgive our sins, but in power to inspire and to rule our lives. And remember that every act of self-discipline, of which no one in this world may know, is known and seen and registered by Christ Himself, and is a link in the chain that binds us to His own life-giving and sustaining presence.

Faith, Prayer, Self-discipline—and lastly Sacrament. If in the first three our will rises to God, then in the fourth God Himself comes down to us, and His Spirit passes within us. I think, of course, especially of the deepest and most wonderful Sacrament of unity with the Living Christ, the Holy Communion.

Surely if any man believes that he runs the risk of being a failure in God's creation, unless somehow or other he lays hold of and brings into his own life the strong life of the Son of Man—if he knows that *this* is the appointed means by which the life of the Son of Man is communicated to him, then his Communions cannot be merely a privilege, they become something more, a necessity. To such a man the acts of his Communion will be not isolated acts of Christian profession but the supreme acts of all his life, the moments in which all his capacities of thought, of imagination, of desire, of will, are raised to their utmost point of intensity, because there he knows that they meet and mingle with the perfect life of Jesus Christ.

Finally, if by faith, prayer, self-discipline and Sacrament we are "abiding in Christ," then we shall bear fruit with the simplicity and inevitableness with which a healthy fig-tree puts forth its figs. We may not always clearly discern the fruit ourselves. Sometimes it is better that we should not; but it will be seen inwardly in the growth of deeper love, strengthened tranquillity, more steadfast joyfulness. It will be seen outwardly in the attractiveness of our example, in the range of our influence, in the perseverance and hopefulness of the service of our fellow-men. This is the bearing of fruit wherein, as our Lord tells us, the Father is glorified. On such a life the Creator, looking down, can see that it is good, and can rejoice in what He has made. Is it not a wonderful thought, almost more wonderful than we can dare to conceive, that my life might become a joy to God Who gave it? "Man's chief end," in the noble words of the Scottish Catechism, "is to glorify God and to enjoy Him for ever." Would not the words be even nobler if they were "to give him joy for ever"? To give joy to God—this is surely the most uplifting and inspiring ambition of life.

THE UNJUST STEWARD

THE UNJUST STEWARD

S. Luke xvi. 1-13

I. A STORY OF WORLDLY ACUTENESS

THIS is a parable which excessive literalism has turned into a maze of subtleties. It has indeed difficulties of its own; but these have been magnified and complicated by a perverted industry which has attempted to extort the most fantastic theories out of every clause. A list of the hundreds of interpretations which during all these centuries have gathered round and entangled in obscurity this parable of the unjust steward is a pathetic record of wasted ingenuity—pathetic, because, it represents such a pitiable abuse of the right reverence which is due to all the words of Jesus. Here, more perhaps than in any other parable the

simplest will be found to be at once the
clearest and the deepest explanation. It
seems plain that our Lord was using a story
of worldly acuteness—a story perhaps which
He had heard in ordinary talk—to teach a
lesson of spiritual prudence. The details of
the steward's clever fraud are of no intrinsic
importance: our Lord makes no comment
on them. He merely takes the man's foresight and promptitude—wicked as they were
in their application—as an illustration of
qualities which have a necessary place in
the spiritual life.

II. GOD OR MAMMON

The concluding words give the real key
to the interpretation of the parable: "Ye
cannot serve God and Mammon." The test
of every man's real value is his answer to
the question—What is the ultimate aim of
your life? Tell me what you are really
living for and I will tell you what you are.
In the last resort, there are but two answers
to that supreme question: the one, God; the

other, Mammon. The aim of life must be
finally either the service of self or the service of God. Most men, capable of asking
themselves the question, avoid and postpone
the answer. But while their thought delays,
their life moves: and its main movement
gives the answer. Every man's life—whatever his theories may be—is gradually set-
tling down into a final answer. To succeed
is to look that answer fairly in the face and
choose and concentrate all one's energies
upon it. To fail, is to avoid it, or, worse
still, to adopt sometimes one answer, sometimes the other. Divided service has always the doom of failure and futility upon
it. He who—in the common way of speaking—tries to "make the best of both worlds"
makes nothing really of either. He merely
loses his chance of enjoying either himself
or God. If the unjust steward had hesitated in carrying out his crime, had allowed
scruples of conscience to hamper and hinder
him, he would have failed hopelessly—he
would have lost both the stewardship to
which he had been unfaithful and the

friends whom he had tried by his trick to
secure. His only chance was to be prompt,
thorough, unscrupulous; and he succeeded.
Therefore his "lord commended the unrighteous steward because he had done
prudently; for the sons of this world are
for their own generation wiser, more pru-
dent, than the sons of the light." That is,
with reference to their own real standard
of life, their own choice of its main motive,
once they have made the choice, their success depends on the determination with
which they act upon it. Because they
recognize this fact, and allow no scruples
to deter them, no half-heartedness and fear-
fulness to trouble them, they win their object. And thus, in their own chosen line,
they are an example of prudence to the
"sons of the light" in theirs. If these sons
of the light really mean to choose God as
their Master, and His service as the aim of
their life, they should be just as whole-
hearted, decided, and courageous. If they,
consciously or unconsciously, try to make
terms for themselves and their own desires,

or to make compromises with the "world," then they are doomed to a double failure. They will fail to enjoy Mammon because their service of it will be spoiled by the scruples and rebukes of conscience. They will fail to enjoy God, because their service of Him will be spoiled by their indulgence of alien desires.

In teaching this lesson, the parable of the unjust steward has a striking modern parallel in Browning's poem, "The Statue and the Bust." That poem has often caused the same difficulties, it enforces the same truth. The two lovers are condemned because they had not the courage and whole-heartedness to stake all for the fulfilment of their love. Let me quote the words in which the poet points his moral:

> "Let a man contend to the uttermost,
>   For his life's set prize, be what it will!
> The counter our lovers staked was lost
> As surely as if it were lawful coin;
> And the sin I impute to each frustrate ghost
> Is—the unlit lamp and the ungirt loin,
> Though the end in sight was a vice, I say,
> You of the virtue (we issue join)
> How strive you? *De te, fabula!*"

That is just our Lord's warning to us who wish to be the "sons of the light," the servants of God. "Concerning you is the parable: how are *you* striving in your life's aim? Are you, for your generation—with reference to your professed purpose—showing anything like the foresight, the decisiveness, the tenacity of the unjust steward? But for *your* success these qualities are just as necessary as for his." It is a truth strangely forgotten but abundantly verified by experience, that if it is worth while to be religious at all, it is worth while to be religious "out and out." That is, after all —so the parable teaches us—common-sense, prudence.

III. THE SECRET OF RELIGIOUS SUCCESS

The success, then, the happiness, of religion depends upon its thoroughness. A half-heart in religion means a heavy heart. Why is it that so many of us who have set out upon the way of Christian discipleship move with steps so languid and eyes so dull, find on the road so much mere struggle and toil, so little freedom and joy? Is it not because we are not yet in our heart of hearts wholly given over to the service of God: because we are really keeping something back in our self-surrender? On the other hand, why is it that others, tried often even more severely, move along in tranquil joy, with some inner music lightening their march—those of whom Keble beautifully speaks—

> "There are in this loud stunning tide
>   Of human care and crime
> With whom the melodies abide
>   Of the everlasting chime:
> Who carry music in their heart
> Through dusky lane and wrangling mart,
> Plying their daily task with busier feet
> Because their secret souls a holy strain repeat."

It is because their self-surrender has been whole-hearted. They realize our Lord's promise: "There is no man that hath left home, or brethren, or sisters, or mother or father, or children, or lands for My sake

and for the Gospel's sake, but he shall receive a hundredfold now in this time, houses
and brethren and sisters and mothers and
children and lands, with persecutions, and
in the world to come eternal life." The
success of sacrifice is always in proportion
to its completeness. If we wish to serve
God at all we must will to serve Him altogether. As William Law, in his wonderful
"Serious Call," insists with impressive
repetition, we must decide once for all and
never falter in our decision that the one aim
of life is to be "to seek to please God in
everything as the best and happiest thing in
the world." For "no servant can serve two
masters; ye cannot serve God and Mammon."

IV. THE USE OF THE MAMMON OF UNRIGTEOUSNESS

But does this mean that we are to
abandon the world altogether? to treat its
duties, its business, its pursuits, its wealth

as if it were a Mammon so necessarily
unrighteous that we can have no dealings with it? The answer of the parable is,
No. This is the second main key to the interpretation. You will find it in verse 9,
followed and explained by verses 10-13. "I
say unto you, Make to yourselves friends out
of this Mammon of unrighteousness, that
when it shall fail, they may receive you
into the enternal Tabernacles." The most
startling paradox of our Lord's command—
to make friendship for eternity out of this
unrighteous Mammon—itself arrests the attention. It is as if He said, "Do not suppose
that because this Mammon is itself unrighteous you can despise or neglect it. On the
contrary you are to use it for your eternal
good: you are to accept your use of it as a
test of your faithfulness. Taken as a master, followed as in itself an all-sufficient object of life, it is unrighteous; but used as
a servant, as an instrument for realizing the
glory of God, it is capable of providing you
with resources of eternal value." The
parable is a rebuke of a false "other world-

liness." Business, money, position—these
are opportunities entrusted to us as stew-
ards, for which we have to give an account
to our Maker. The parable shows us the
place which they have in the service of
God.

V. A DISCIPLINE OF FIDELITY

They furnish a discipline of fidelity. "He
that is faithful in a very little is faithful
also in much, and he that is unrighteous in
a very little, is unrighteous also in much.
If therefore ye have not been faithful in
the unrighteous Mammon, who will commit
to your trust the true riches?" (verses
10-12). To persons of a certain temperament, it is comparatively easy to serve God
in fine feelings, in devout meditations, in
eager attendance at religious services, in
conspicuous acts of charity. But it is a far
severer test to serve God in "serving
tables," in doing daily business thoroughly
and cheerfully (as Stevenson says, "letting

cheerfulness abound with industry"), in keeping a watchful eye on the relations of expenditure and income, in paying small debts promptly, in discharging with eager care the little, often irksome, duties of home and family life. But these are just the lesser duties by which our fitness for the greater duties is disciplined and tested. No man, who has accepted or continues in a post of business can plead as an excuse for neglecting it that he is engaged in religious duties. His primary religious duty is to do his business as well as he can. No woman, who is charged with the task of keeping her house, can plead as an excuse for leaving it untidy or uncomfortable, or restless, that she is busy with "church work." Her primary church work is to be the centre of a happy home. The testimony to the real thoroughness of our religion, which is at once the hardest to earn and the most rigorously exacted by the observant world, is the testimony borne to it by our workaday character. Let me give a very simple illustration. Suppose the question is—"Has this young man in business the real signs of a vocation to the ministry?" Testimonials are at hand as to his devotion to church services, his eloquent addresses to children and the like. But we remain uncertain. Then a letter comes from his employers: "We gladly bear testimony to the integrity and efficiency with which Mr. A. has done his work. We entrusted him lately with a special task requiring great application and persistence; and we were entirely satisfied with the result." That letter is of decisive value. It gives to the others just the assurance which otherwise would have been wanting. For—"He that is faithful in a very little is faithful also in much." Nay, we may go further. There will always be something desultory, shifting, inconsistent, untrustworthy in the religious emotions or thoughts or labours which have not this solid foundation in the honest and faithful doing of a day's work. You may, for example, almost assume that a man who shows want of method in his business affairs will somehow and somewhere show want of *will* in his religion—want of honest, single-eyed consistency. A sure, steadfast, progressive spiritual life cannot be combined with slack and careless business habits. "If ye have not been faithful in the unrighteous Mammon, who will commit to your trust the true riches?"

Once again we may summon an English poet to enforce the lesson of this parable. You may remember the noble words in which Tennyson's King Arthur rebukes his knights because they forsook their vows to wander in quest of the vision of the Holy Grail and vindicates his own steadfastness at the post of duty.

"And some among you hold that if the King
  Had seen the sight he would have sworn the vow:
  Not easily, seeing that the King must guard
  That which he rules, and is but as the hind
  To whom space of land is given to plough,
  Who may not wander from the allotted field
  Before his work is done; but being done,
  Let visions of the night or of the day
  Come as they will: and many a time they come.
  Until this earth he walks on seems not earth,
  This light that strikes his eyeball is not light,

This air that smites his forehead is not air
But vision—yea, his very hand and foot—
In moments when he feels he cannot die,
And knows himself no vision to himself,
Nor the high God a vision, nor that One
Who rose again."

His faithfulness to his immediate duty
won for him the "true riches."

VI. A FRIEND IN THE ETERNAL TABERNACLES

"Mammon" is to be used, secondly, as a
means of providing resources which will
stand us in good stead when we pass from
this present scene into the eternal world.
The unjust steward knew that his gains
were gone past recovery, but his astuteness
provided him with friends who would save
him, in the hour of his dismissal, from beggary. We too know that an hour will come
when all our Mammon—our money, comforts, successes, position — will "fail."
Naked we came into the world, and naked
we shall leave it. Dust we are and to dust

we shall return. We cannot take with us
beyond the grave our business or the success
it may have gained for us, our money or the
pleasures it may have brought. But we can
take the good we may have won or done.
The moral qualities with which our use of
Mammon may have strengthened and disciplined our character, the kindness it may
have enabled us to show, the compassion it
may have enabled us to realize, the self-
sacrifice it may have enabled us to practise,
the strength and cheer it may have enabled
us to give to our fellows—these are secured
for us, waiting as it were in the eternal
world to speak for us, and to welcome us.
It is well for us to contemplate that solitary
journey which awaits us all when death has
knocked at the door and summoned us
forth. Let me quote the words of Samuel
Rutherford: "Take with you in your journey what you may carry with you, your conscience, faith, hope, patience, meekness,
goodness, brotherly kindness; for such
wares as these are of great price in the high
and new country whither ye go. As for

other things which are but this world's vanity and trash . . . ye will do best not to carry them with you. Ye found them here; leave them here." Mammon itself, after all, is "but this world's vanity and trash." It shall fail—that is certain. It has no value or credit beyond the grave. But the good we do with it—that is laid up for us in the new life to which we pass, so that we can draw upon it when we shall be stripped of all our possessions. We shall meet it as a friend ready to receive us into the eternal tabernacles.

THE UNPROFITABLE SERVANTS

THE UNPROFITABLE SERVANTS

S. Luke xvii. 7-10

I. THE SENSE OF DUTY

THIS parable cannot, in comparison with many others, claim to rank as one of the most important. It is very short; its relation to the context is hard to construe. But it deals so directly with a characteristic British temperament that I venture to select its main lesson for special consideration. We need not spend time in discussing whether it was meant to be a caution to the disciples, lest they should presume upon their possession of the power of faith (verse 6); or whether it was meant to be a description of the Jewish religion of works in contrast with the new religion of faith. For there is no difficulty in understanding the

main lesson which our Lord enforced. It is
that the only limit to the servant's duty is
his master's will; that there is no point at
which he can choose for himself to claim
that he has done enough and is entitled to
his ease; that the servant is always a debtor
of service, the master is never a debtor of
reward. And it is this lesson of which our
British race stands in very special need. Is
it too much to say that our Lord's conclusion comes as a surprise, that if it had been
spoken by the average upright conscientious
Englishman, it would have run, "We have
done that which was our duty to do; therefore we can claim to be profitable
servants"?

For our race worships this sense of duty.
It is our national idol. When on the great
day of Trafalgar Nelson flung out his brave
motto to the breeze, "England expects every
man to do his duty," he was unfolding the
national faith. In any audience, at any
time, in any part of the world, the words
go straight home to the heart of the nation.
England expects every man to do his duty—

so speaks our national conscience. England
gets what she expects—this we would fain
make our national boast. May we not in
some degree claim that the boast is just?
Still, in the main, it is true—God grant it
may remain true—that you *can* expect the
average Englishman to do his duty. Our
whole public life rests upon that expectation. We need no despotism to set us in the
right road; we do not look to any central
office of experts to keep us straight. We entrust large and free powers of self-govern-
ment to the average conscience of the average man. And our whole English public
life would go to pieces unless the national
faith had some warrant in fact. But it is, for
the most part, abroad, where men confront
other and less civilized nations, that this
English ideal is best tested. In the public
service at any rate the "white man's burden"
is sustained by the sense of duty. A Viceroy
of India said the other day that in the midst
of his manifold labours he was sustained by
a thrill of pride in the thought that a sense
of duty, unfailing, all pervading, was the

real motive power of the vast machinery of
Indian Government. Deep down, unex-
pressed, but shown by faithful acts, there is
in most Englishmen a quiet determination
to be just, to keep his word, to do his duty.
Nay, may we not go further? In his mind
the word "duty" surely stands for something deeper than it seems to express. Suspicious as he is of emotion, reserved in
speech, duty often means to him, God. It
is not merely that his duty is his God, but
that his God speaks to him in his duty, and
there is an instinct of reverence for God in
his obedience to it. As Tennyson says in that
great ode which is as it were a Psalm of
Duty—

He that, ever following her commands,
On, with toil of heart and knees and hands,
   Through the long gorge to the far light has won
His path upward and prevailed,
Shall find the toppling crags of Duty scaled
Are close upon the shining table-lands
   To which our God Himself is Moon and Sun."

Yet in spite of all this truth there con-
fronts us this hard saying of our Lord: "We

are unprofitable servants; we have done that which was our duty to do."

It is plain that our Lord discerns something wanting, some germ of danger in this contented devotion to duty. What is it? Is it not this—that duty, as it is commonly conceived, apart from its heroic aspect, tends to become simply what is expected or recognized by some limited and conventional standard? It is of this lower, but far more common type of duty, that our Lord is speaking in the parable. And here it is that we touch the defects of our British virtue; for in asking himself, "What is my duty?" the Englishman is apt to find an answer in the standard of public opinion by which he is surrounded. Duty too often means the average expectation in any given condition of life. Thus, at school, when he is a boy, the Englishman follows with ready and resolute determination all the rules and traditions of school life and school morality. He is half-ashamed and half-afraid to go beyond. In the army or the navy he will say, as I have so often heard said to me, "I am bound to do what the service requires, and to do it well; but when it comes to my private conduct, that is a matter entirely of my own concern." In business the code of right and wrong becomes too easily what is done by the average good firm. Is it not, on the lips of men we meet, a frequent apology, "I do what is expected of a man in my position"? He refuses, he scorns, to go beneath the accepted opinion of his class; but he is afraid to rise above it.

II. THE LIMITATIONS OF THE SENSE OF DUTY

There are two ways in which this real defectiveness of the sense of duty shows itself. The one is that it limits and narrows the life. It keeps it, indeed, within fixed and safe barriers, but the safety and the ease are had at the cost of progress. You see the average good Englishman, upright and honourable. You like and respect him, yet, somehow, he suggests an arrested possibility. He is so suspicious of enthusi-

asm that he becomes incapable of it; so
distrustful of ideals that he would rather
do without them. He prefers the safety of
the beaten track to the perils and glories of
the open hill.   He is content to say, "Well,
at least, we are profitable servants: we have
done that which was our duty to do." You
like him, you respect him, you trust him:

> "Only he knows not God,
>   Nor all that chivalry of His
>   The soldier saints who row on row
>   Burn upward each to his point of bliss."

And the second defect which goes with
this common conception of duty is a certain
self-satisfaction. The standard is satisfied:
the requirement is met; the expectation is
answered. What more can be asked? Thus
we notice a certain smoothness of compla-
cency sinking down upon the average dutiful man. How hard and impenetrable that
smooth surface may become they best know
who have tried to approach such a man
at the close of life with the strange
memory of the cross or with the appeal for

some sign of penitence. For ten who will
say on reviewing the course of their life,
"We have done that which was our duty to
do," there is barely one who will add, "We
are unprofitable servants." When we see
the narrowness and self-satisfaction that
somehow or other spoils the dutiful man, we
realize how near the best of us may come to
the Pharisee of the New Testament.
"There is always," said an eminent French
critic, "there is always a touch of the
Pharisee in the good Englishman." That,
too, is a hard saying. We resent it. Is it
harder than the saying of our Lord in the
parable? The spirit of pharisaism is wide.
It ranges from the lowest forms in which
instinctively we dislike it up to the highest,
in which it comes to have even a certain
attractiveness. When we meet the Pharisee
who says in the tone of his voice or the
posture of his figure, "Thank God, I am
not as other men are, or even as this publican," we know that his spirit is fundamentally wrong. But when we meet a rich
young man, eager to do what is right, asking

quite sincerely, "What must I do to inherit
eternal life?" and then saying with honest
frankness, "All these commandments have
I kept from my youth up," then we like
him, we admire him. It is indeed in the
rich young ruler of the New Testament that
the most attractive type of English character finds itself, as it were, mirrored, and
there it is both loved and judged. "Then
Jesus, beholding him, loved him, and said
unto him, One thing thou lackest: go thy
way, sell whatsoever thou hast, and give to
the poor, and thou shalt have treasure in
heaven; and come, take up thy cross and
follow Me."

III. THE NEED OF AN INWARD IDEAL

What then do we need to redeem this
great sense of duty from its dangers? We
need an inward personal ideal rising ever
above the conventional standards of expectation. The inner spirit must refuse to accept limits from the outward circumstances
of class or profession, but move past them

on a quest of its own. It is thus that the spirit keeps its liberty, and moulds and masters the conditions by which it is surrounded, instead of allowing itself to be mastered and moulded by them. And where there is liberty there is the possibility of progress. It is only by the power of a free inward ideal that character expands and grows. Moreover, thus capable of progress, such a character is incapable of self-satisfaction. A man who is determined in his own inward life to be the best that he can be can never fold his hands and say complacently, "I am a profitable servant; I have done that which it was my duty to do." If we can say "all these commandments have I kept," we are only at the best "not far from the Kingdom of God." As soon as we take the path of ceaseless effort and sacrifice, we enter within it.

IV. THE INFINITE CLAIM OF GOD

The sense of duty to be complete needs the recognition of the infinite claim of an infinite God. We come back to the old truth—"The soul is made for God and can find its rest only in Him." That quest of the inward ideal, that impatience with every stage of attainment, is God's drawing of the soul into fellowship with Himself. It may be that the spirit in its own inward journey realizes the need of God, and through the earnestness of that sense of need finds its way to Him. It may be that God Himself using some experience or influence of a man's life, lays hold upon him and bids him go forth to follow His leading to the end. In either case, it is this recognition of the infinite claim of an infinite God which redeems and transforms the sense of duty. There can then be no danger of halting and stopping short, for God's claims summon us to a never-ending progress towards union with Himself. There can be no danger of self-satisfaction, for God's own perfection is the goal, and at every stage we realize how far short of it we come. The more we realize that God Himself is the End for which He has given

us our being the more conscious we become
of the presence of rival aims and of our
manifold surrenders to them; and thus the
sense of imperfection deepens into the sense
of sin.   It is our sin which entangles and
impedes the soul in its true movement towards God and which bars the way to God's
gracious movement towards us, and thus
prevents the union of God and man for
which we were made.   But there is nothing
in the mere *sense* of sin which avails either
to remove its burden from the conscience or
to break its power over the will.   It is here
that one welcomes with ever renewed
thankfulness the knowledge that One in
whom God and man were perfectly at one
obtained, by a "full and sufficient" sacrifice
of obedience, forgiveness for all sin, and has
brought into our life the strength of a vic-
torious will of good; and that if only a man
by faith and prayer and sacrament and self-
sacrifice keeps hold upon Him, he is assured alike of that pardon and of that
power.   It is this encompassing security
which brings into the long struggle out of

self to God a sense of sureness and of peace.
Being cleansed from sin we can serve God
with a quiet mind.

I. THE PERFECT SENSE OF DUTY

What we need to redeem and perfect the
sense of duty is to remember that beyond
what any standard of human opinion expects, beyond what "England expects," remains what God expects; that God can expect nothing less than the union of our
mind and will with His; that this expectation can only be met by that entire sacrifice
of body, soul and spirit which is after all
our reasonable service; that to this Divine
expectation we are kept true by the sense of
our own unworthiness, which leads us ever
to plead the atonement and to accept the
grace of Christ our Lord. It is only to him
who honestly confesses "we are unprofitable
servants; we have only done that which was
our duty to do," that, after long service, is
assured the Master's praise: "Well done,
good and faithful servant."

I cannot better sum up the thought given to us by this parable than by quoting the words, adapted from the ancient hymn of Cleanthes, in which a great and typical Englishman, William Stubbs, Bishop of Oxford, a man reserved in speech, almost morbid in his English dislike of emotional display, devoted to the sense of duty, reveals the secret of his humility and of his strength—

"Lead me, Almighty Father, Spirit, Son,
    Whither Thou wilt, I follow, no delay,
My will is Thine, and even had I none,
    Grudging obedience still I will obey.
Faint-hearted, fearful, doubtful if I be,
Gladly or sadly I will follow Thee.

"Into the land of righteousness I go,
    The footsteps thither Thine and not my own,
Jesu, Thyself the way, alone I know,
    Thy will be mine, for other have I none.
Unprofitable servant though I be,
Gladly or sadly let me follow Thee."

THE FRIEND AT MIDNIGHT AND THE UNJUST JUDGE

THE FRIEND AT MIDNIGHT AND
THE UNJUST JUDGE

S. Luke xi. 5-8 *and* xviii. 1-8

I. FROM MAN TO GOD

THESE two parables are closely akin. They make the same comparison and contrast between what we expect of human nature even in unworthy types and what we may expect of God. They draw the same inference that God in His goodness will not come short of that expectation which we have of our fellowmen even in their unworthiness. They enforce this same lesson that in order to make sure of God's answers our prayers must be intense and persistent.

Consider that comparison and contrast and the inference which is drawn from it. As in the parable of the unjust steward, our Lord chooses the example not of the best but of the most ordinary, indeed unworthy, men to emphasize His argument. He illustrates the point of His own saying, "If ye then *being evil* know how to give good gifts unto your children, how much more shall your Heavenly Father give good things to them that ask Him." Here He takes certain men "being evil," the churlish friend and the unjust judge, shows the conduct of which under certain circumstances they are capable, and asks whether under similar circumstances God Himself, the Loving and the Righteous, will not prove to be at least as generous and just. In this, we might almost say surprising, way, our Lord gives His sanction to the belief that we can learn of God from what we know of man; that at least the moral attributes of love, justice, mercy, sympathy in God are not different from, but only infinitely transcend, what we know these attributes to be in man. In the education of Israel the inspired prophets had indeed rebuked men for transferring their own ignorant and partial thoughts to God. They had held up to scorn the false gods clothed with the qualities of ordinary human nature. They insisted that God's ways and thoughts are not as the thoughts and ways of man; for they far transcended the compass of man's mind and imagination. But these very champions of God's transcendence never hesitated to represent Him as having towards His people the feelings of love, of jealous care, of righteous indignation, which a father has towards his children or a husband towards his wife, or a judge towards the wrongdoer. Even in the pagan deification of the qualities which men most admired in their own fellows, still more in some of the deeper thoughts of the religions of India, we can see the instinct of man's spirit which believes that the Divine Being has at least that affinity with man which makes intercourse between them possible. Philosophy insists that the mind of which the universe is the expression cannot be *less* rational in its methods than the mind of man. Religious thought at its highest point insists that if Love is the noblest quality of man there must be in God a Love not less but infinitely more noble and true. Indeed, if the evolution of the universe reaches its highest stage in man, there would be an arrest, an inexplicable failure, in the upward movement unless "in completed man began anew a tendency to God"—unless manhood at its highest could rise to God and find itself fulfilled there. Thus the Incarnation, though, as we say, "miraculous" in the method of its coming, is no mere isolated marvel. It is God's supreme vindication of man's inevitable instinct of expectation that man can hold communion with God, because there is that in God which is in common with man. The Incarnation, indeed, lifts the thought to a higher and truer standpoint: so that it does not rise from man to God so much as descend from God to man. In the light of that revelation the higher attributes of man are seen to be the reflections in him of the Perfection of God; they are the tokens not only of manhood in God but rather of Godhead in man.

But such thoughts carry us far beyond the purposes of these simple papers. And after all, the teaching of Jesus here, as always, is practical not speculative. His object is simply to impress upon men the conviction that the kindness and justice which they expect of their fellows, even the least worthy, they may with infinitely greater confidence expect of their Father in Heaven. It is perhaps worth while to pause here to notice at least two ways—one of presumption, the other of distrust—in which we are very apt to neglect this truth.

II. THE JUSTICE OF GOD

In the first place we forget it often in presuming upon the forbearance of Divine justice. Consider seriously the course of our inward life—the acts repeated over and

over again of disobedience to what we know
clearly to be God's will, the manifold be-
trayals of trusts which He has committed
to us, the failure of service and losses of opportunity through our sloth and self-indulgence. Is there any earthly master or even
father, with any ordinary sense of justice,
who could pass by such conduct as if it mat-
tered nothing? And will God, the All-holy
and All-just, be less careful and exacting
than an ordinary man? Yet do we not go on
with these secret sins and surrenders and self-
indulgences, as if somehow they involved no
serious consequences? We ought rather to
be convinced, and to act upon the conviction,
that unless our penitence is constant and sincere and our efforts of amendment are increasingly strenuous, these apparently undis-
turbed acts or habits of disobedience must
all the while be bringing upon us some real
spiritual punishment which will be revealed
if not here then hereafter. This would only
be *right* if we were dealing with an earthly
master, judge, or father. And "shall not
the Judge of all the earth do right?"

III. THE FATHERHOOD OF GOD

In the second place we are often apt to distrust the reality of the Divine Fatherhood. There are mysteries in God's ordering of the world which we cannot fathom. They are and must be a heavy strain upon our faith in His Fatherly will. Yet behind even these mysteries, in the ultimate motive and issue of things, there can be nothing finally inconsistent with all that we mean by fatherhood. And when we pass from these mysteries of Providence to the direct relations between the spirit of man and God, there we are to hold to that truth of fatherhood with quite immediate and un-faltering certainty. Yet are there not many good people who, for example in the morbid scrupulosity of their conscience, or in deciding the rival claims of mercy and ecclesiastical rules, or in considering the fate of the heathen, of the ignorant, of the vast masses who have had no chance of worthy life, seem to hesitate in this sure and simple trust? Again, we can think of systems of religion—not only in past history—limiting, by rigorist views of Church order, or precise doctrines as to "predestination," God's own power of saving His own children—systems which, for all their imposing aray of logic, have missed the essential mark of truth — consistency with the Fatherhood of God. And as that truth is the final test of religious theory, so it is the final stay and security of the soul. We cannot be too simple in our grasp of it. Often, under the strain of sorrow, perplexity, doubt, other anchors in which we trusted slip; but if the last anchor holds— this faith that below all depths and above all heights stand eternally the Will, the Wisdom, the Love of a Father—then we shall not drift; we shall be secure till the storm is past.

> "Then was I as a child that cries,
> But crying knows his father near."

IV.   THE IMPORTUNITY OF PRAYER

This, then, is the point of our Lord's comparison—the Divine Father of all will

surely not come short of the grudging
friend, nor the All-righteous One of the
unjust judge. We pass to the main lesson
which the two parables teach. It is given
in the preface to that of the unjust judge,
"that men ought always to pray and not
to faint"; and in the conclusion to that of
the friend at midnight, "I say unto you,
Ask and it shall be given unto you; Seek
and ye shall find; Knock and it shall be
opened unto you." It is the two-fold
lesson—that prayer must be patient and
persistent and that such prayer is sure of its
answer.

In both parables, the stress is laid upon
this importunity of prayer. It need scarcely
be pointed out that the stress is not laid
upon the reluctance with which the prayer
is answered. God is always more ready
to hear than we are to pray, more willing
to give than we are to receive. The point of
of our Lord's appeal is simply that if importunity of prayer availed to overcome the
reluctance of the grudging friend or of the
unjust judge, how much more will it avail

to secure the willing response of a loving
and just Father? But, even so, is it not a
hard saying that such a Father should, as it
were, *require* this importunity of prayer
before He answers? It is a natural question
often asked. Well, consider the human
analogy. Does a wise father shower gifts
upon his child without waiting for some
sign that the child really deserves them, is
able to appreciate and use them? If he
docs he only spoils his child. And would
not one sign of such desire and capacity be
the urgency of the child's entreaties? Thus
importunity of prayer is the sign for which
God's loving wisdom waits of the sincerity
of our desire for His gifts, and of the fitness
of our character to receive them. It is the
evidence of desire. If our prayer be formal,
languid, intermittent, our desire cannot be
real and deep. And urgency of prayer is
the evidence of fitness of character to receive. As our Lord implies in His own
comment on the parable of the unjust
judge, it is a test of that co-operating faith
which is the condition of receiving His

grace. He only will pray with persistence who really believes that God is, and that He is the rewarder of them that diligently seek him. Above all, prayer is the test of our willing submission to God's will. It is the acknowledgment of that dependence upon Him, the expression of that obedience, which is the essence of true freedom. It is the primary and indispensable act of sonship. For all prayer is based upon one prayer—"Thy will be done." It is in its deepest truth the effort, not chiefly to obtain our own desires, but to bring them into the Will of God and leave them there in perfect trust. Thus the importunity of prayer is a token of the resoluteness and strenuousness with which our will is set towards God's. To him whose will is thus proved to be in line with God's will, God can safely entrust His gifts.

The lesson of the two parables is thus one aspect of that which is taught in the striking words—"The Kingdom of Heaven suffereth violence, and the violent take it by force." For that Kingdom, just because it

is the Kingdom of God, is set on high, and
the ascent to it is steep and narrow. To
reach it is a task beyond the compass of
a feeble, listless, timorous spirit. It can
only be achieved by strenuousness, intensity,
and courage. In this upward struggle,
increasing difficulty must be met by increasing determination. If asking be not
answered, then we must seek; if seeking
be unavailing, then we must knock—knock
with the energy of one whose whole will is
set on effecting an entrance. Archbishop
Trench fitly quotes the great words of
Dante:

> "Fervent love
> And lively hope, with violence assail
> The kingdom of the heavens, and overcome
> The will of the Most High: not in such sort
> As man prevails o'er man; but conquers it
> Because 'tis willing to be conquered, still,
> Though conquered, by its mercy conquering."

The Law of Struggle is only the Law of
Love as it is manifested on the steeps of
the Hill of Life. There, Love would not
be love unless it tested, braced, and quick-
ened the free spirit of man—gave him spurs

for his ascent. On the summit, but not till then, we shall see the same guiding Love transform the Law of Struggle into the Law of Rest. It is not, therefore, the sternness but the Love of God, or rather it is His Love manifested in sternness, which requires from His children the importunity of prayer.

Such prayer, then, is assured of its answer. God hears it: its persistence, so to say, forces an entrance into His audience-chamber: and the more earnest the prayer, the nearer the spirit penetrates to God. "He heareth us: and if we know that He heareth us, we know that we have the petitions which we have asked of Him." The answer is not always what we asked or expected. In the parable of the friend at midnight, the response was fuller than the request—it was not three loaves only but as many as were needed. But it is not always so. There are often delays and surprises in the answer. But the one thing sure is that earnest prayer secures that answer which the absolute Love and Wisdom of God know to be the truest and best. The man of the world scoffs at this trust of the Christian: "If you get what you ask, you say it is an answer to your prayer: if you don't, you still say your prayer is answered; what then is the use of praying at all?" But the philosophy of the kingdom of God is deeper than the logic of the world. The Christian knows that what he really wishes is only what God wills, that God chooses to wait for the evidence of free submission to that will before it is done: and that this evidence is given in prayer. Let us then have a heart of courage and confidence in our prayers. "Men ought always to pray and not to faint." It is by the wings of prayer that life is lifted to God. If these wings are slack, the spirit will grow faint in its flight. If they are strong, and beat the air with a persistent force, then, through all the buffeting blasts of difficulty and perplexity, the spirit will keep its course in patience, impelled and sustained by the will of God.

V. THE NEED OF INTERCESSORY PRAYER

There are some special features in each of the two parables as to which a few words may be added. In the parable of the Friend at Midnight, the request is made on behalf of another—of the traveller who arrives unexpectedly. We need not dwell on the possible occult meanings which subtlety of interpretation may extract out of the relations of the traveller and his host. But we shall be true to the spirit of the parable if we learn from it the need of earnest intercessory prayer in our dealings with men with whom in any way our lot is cast. No one can look back upon his life without marvelling at the mystery of human intercourse. People, we say, "come into our lives," from all sorts of life-journeys, unexpected, uninvited. It is an experience which will become more and more common as modern life grows in complexity. There is a widespread restlessness of mind and of body which drives men forth from the settled homes of custom. There are more

travellers in the region of the spirit, as over
the face of the globe, than there used to be.
May we not say that now in every circle of
friends, nay in every home, there is a society
of travellers, each engaged in some journey
of his own, of which the others are perhaps
ignorant, and in which they cannot follow
him? If there is any human hospitality in
our characters, such travellers will often
arrive at our doors, unexpected, perhaps
out of the unknown, when we are least
ready for them, asking us for strength, for
refreshment, for rest in their journey. Here
arrives one in great moral perplexity asking
for advice; another, in the lonely wandering of sorrow, asking for comfort; another,
who has lost his way in doubt, asking for
light; or, in the words of S. Augustine,
"perchance there cometh some wearied
friend of thine, who, worn out amid all the
desires and the poverty of the world, comes
to thee as to a Christian and says, 'Give me
an account of it, make me a Christian.'"
May we not say that an unexpected traveller is knocking at the door when the mother

hears a sudden and troubled question come
from the lips of her child; or when a man
discerns in quiet talk a new note of sadness
or of entreaty in the voice of his old friend?
And alas! often when the traveller comes
we "have nothing to set before him." We
are taken unawares: our minds have been
asleep: our own spirit is tired: our stock
of provender, always scanty enough for our
own soul's need, is for the moment exhausted. What are we to do? We cannot
turn the traveller from our door: but it is
useless to keep him waiting with barren
words: he has come for bread. In such a
strait—and who is there who does not or
may not find himself in it?—there is but one
thing to do. We must go at once—at the
very midnight of the unexpected arrival—
to the Friend in Whose treasures there is
provision for the needs of every human
soul. We must rouse Him by the earnestness of our prayer, and ask Him to give the
bread which we lack. I know by abundant
experience that it has made all the difference in helping those who have asked for

help whether or not one has immediately gone with their need to God. One who exercised great influence for good at Cambridge has even said that he almost gave up much talking to those whom he wished to help in order that he might devote the time to what he found far more effective—much praying for them. It is indeed best to *have* something of our own which we can set before these life-travellers who come to us —a sympathy trained to be discerning, a frankness which is willing for another's sake to speak of self, or—in these days especially —some real knowledge of the Christian Faith, and some ability to give at least that reason for it which has convinced ourselves. But even then we have need of prayer that we may present what we have in the way and with the tact which will best commend it, above all that we may secure the aid of that Holy Spirit without Whom no words of ours can go home to another's heart or mind or conscience. Constant prayerfulness keeps the spirit in readiness for these sudden demands and enables it to meet them,

It was said of the Spanish mystic, Juan de Avila, that "he seemed always as if he had just issued forth from a long and fervent prayer, and his very look was enough to edify men." The spirit of prayer is the secret of influence. And remember, once again, that prayer for others must be insistent and persistent. It is the mother who prays with the constancy of a Monica who wins her son for God. It is the man who inwardly wrestles with God for his friends, who becomes a Prince in influence over them and prevails.

VI. THE CRY OF THE TEMPTED

In the parable of the Unjust Judge, the entreaty of the widow is a cry of urgent personal need — "Avenge me of mine adversary." Is it not also the cry of many a soul under the pressure of relentless temptation? Many of us know that beyond the temptations to which every man is exposed there are some which attack us in our special temperaments, histories, circumstances, with special frequency and ferocity. Doubtless, alas! it is because long ago we surrendered the first ramparts that the attack is now constant in the very citadel of the heart. But even when we have come to repudiate the suggestions of evil, they still beset and torment us. And when we think of the ingenuity of the assault, of the insight which it discloses into the weak points of our armoury of character, we are driven to the conclusion that the enemy is as personal as, and far more intelligent than, ourselves. The prayer, "Deliver us from the Evil One," interprets our experience better than the prayer, "Deliver us from evil." Sore beset and worried with the ceaseless conflict, we cry out, "Thou God to Whom vengeance belongeth show Thyself—avenge me of mine adversary." If this struggle be our lot, let us take heart from the lesson of the parable. "Shall not God avenge His elect which cry day and night unto Him?" Both the true reading and the exact meaning of the words which follow (verse 7) are uncertain. But we may rightly paraphrase them thus:—Though He seems to hold His vengeance over them under a long delay, yet in truth He will avenge them, and that speedily. In point of time, the delay may seem long—all our life on this side of death we may be in the combat. But in point of fulfilment of God's will for us, the deliverance will come "speedily," that is, at the very moment at which the great Commander, in His plan for our immortal destiny, sees that the time for our release has come. Till then, we have to keep our post. But the time *will* come when God will relieve the guard, and His sentinel can say, "Now lettest Thou Thy servant depart in peace." Meanwhile, our orders are, "Watch and pray." We are to prove our vigilance by the constancy of our prayer. Indeed, even now, persistent prayer will be our best defence. For he who at the very moment of temptation turns at once to God in prayer—"Now, O Lord, now avenge me of mine adversary," cannot, while he is praying, at the same time be yielding. It is in and by the word of prayer that the Sword of the Spirit is kept firmly in his hand.

VII. THE CRY OF THE CHURCH MILITANT

Again, the prayer in the parable is the cry of the "Church Militant here in earth," in its age-long struggle with the "powers of this world." The Church is charged by its Head with the task of overcoming the world by bringing it into subjection to the Kingdom of God. Certainly the victory seems to be far off. The Church in the thick of the battle, say in the midst of one of our great modern cities, seems scarcely to hold its own, much less to prevail, against the forces of evil and indifference. It is easy to despair, at least to give way to depression, to be content with endurance and give up the hope of victory. The one supreme remedy for the Church is to set itself to unremitting intercession with God. It is here that we specially see the providential purpose which has preserved the old Psalms to be the camp-songs of the Christian army. From them, in every variety of tone, the cry is ever rising— "Avenge me of mine adversaries." It is persistence of intercession that alone can keep the Church true to its task, quicken its harassed faith, and sustain its drooping spirit. For if it is thus "instant in prayer," it comes within the promise, "Shall not God avenge His elect which cry day and night unto Him? I tell you that He will avenge them speedily." God knows His own time: it will come, and when it comes, the faithful Church will see the victory once achieved in the hidden spiritual world on the Cross of Christ made manifest before angels and men.

These, no doubt, are bold words, and, as I write them, the warning with which Jesus closes the parable meets the eye. "Nevertheless, when the Son of Man cometh shall He find faith on the earth?" Shall He find His Church after all these centuries of waiting still proving its faith by the fer-

vour of its prayer? Shall He find it
still praying with unfaltering faith, and
steadfast will, in spite of all the evidences
of the power and persistence of evil, "Thy
Kingdom come on earth?" Or shall He
find that its intercessions have become a
mere hollow sound of rhetoric out of which
any real expectation of answer has van-
ished? It is a question which we may well
lay to heart; and rather than give any
confident answer, offer the humble prayer,
"Lord increase our faith."

THE PHARISEE AND THE PUBLICAN

THE PHARISEE AND THE PUBLICAN

S. *Luke* xviii. 9-14

I. THE SENSE OF SIN

OF the parables of our Lord, that of the Pharisee and the Publican is one of the shortest and most searching. It is a picture of the inner and secret life of man, as it is laid bare before the absolute Truth. It teaches a fundamental lesson, which must be known and grasped before any other lesson of the Christian life can be really understood or fruitfully followed. The lesson is that one of the foundations of character must be a personal sense of sin.

Life is the sum of our relationships. Our life is true and right, just in proportion as our relationships with ourselves, our fellows, the world, and God, are right and true. There can be no question that, of all these complex relationships, the deepest and the most important is that in which we stand towards God. He is the unity of all the rest; and, therefore, the very basis of our life, without which it can have no security, is the attitude in which in our inmost souls we stand towards Him. To be wrong there, is to be wrong utterly. It is the one fatal error. To be right there is, ultimately, to be right everywhere. It is the one final truth.

Now we know what our relationship with God ought to be. Our conscience, trained by the long centuries of God's discipline of this race, knows that our relationship with Him is meant to be that of sons living in free independence upon a Father, finding more and more in obedience to Him their perfect freedom, in knowledge of Him their eternal life, in love of Him their all-sufficing peace and joy. That filial union is the true meaning of our life. That is what we are meant to be. The conscience of each one assures us that as a matter of fact, it is not what we are. Something has intervened, has broken and disturbed this unity. It is the force which we call sin. Sin in its essence is self-will, self-satisfaction, the assertion of independence of God. God's will for us—union with Himself—that is our Eden. Self-will—that is our Adam. For "every man is the Adam of his own soul." Union with God—that is life. Separation from God—that is death. And sin is within us as a disease which is gradually, and most certainly alienating us from the life of God and bringing us towards death. We are all infected by it. Therefore, the first step to any recovery of our true life is to recognize both the presence and the gravity of sin. To confess our sin, to be penitent, to be anxious about salvation—that is nothing morbid or unreal; it is only the honesty which faces the fact. It is the first essential of health. No man is healthy, or can be healthy, until he has learned to confess his sin. For without

the sense of sin, we are making a mistake in
the primary relationship of life.   Nothing
can go well with us until we have dealt with
ourselves honestly there.   "If we say that
we have no sin, we deceive ourselves, and
the truth is not in us."

II. OUR LORD'S TREATMENT OF SIN

It is characteristic of our Lord's—shall
we dare to say?—original and most searching treatment of sin, that in the parable
before us He selects as the type of the man
involved in this great mistake not the open
and avowed sinner, not the thoughtless man
of the world, but the conscientious and ex-
emplary professor of religion.   Here is a
man, not only of conspicuous integrity and
probity of life, but a man who gives more
than ordinary signs of his devoutness.   He
fasts twice in the week; he gives a tenth
part of all that he gets to God.   And yet,
this man carries his sin into his very
religion.   His religion—not his mind or his

flesh—but his religion, is the sanctuary of his sin. The sin reveals itself in his very prayer. His prayer is an act of self-congratulation. The real tragedy of the man is that his plight is worse than that of the open and avowed sinner. For his sin is in his very soul. There is no hope for him; for the one great lie—that utter untruthfulness to eternal facts which is involved in any sort of self-satisfaction—is lodged in his inmost spirit.

We turn to the other—the publican; a miserable object, doubtless, a member of a discredited class. We see him standing afar off, with downcast eyes, beating his breast, groaning in the bitterness of his soul, "God, be merciful to me, a sinner." He is conscious that he wishes to be nearer to God, but that he is hopelessly far from Him. He knows that only the pitiful mercy of God can possibly reach and raise him. And yet, just because he is self-condemned and owns his utter dependence upon the mercy of God, for that reason, there is an infinity of hope for him. In his inmost spirit there lies the one great truth. He goes down to his house justified.

There is no question that this way of thinking and speaking is not congenial to our modern religious temperament. We do not naturally think and speak in a severe way about the fact of sin. It is related of that great Christian, Mr. Gladstone, that he was once asked what was the great want of modern life, and that he replied slowly and reflectively—we can almost hear him saying it—"Ah, a sense of sin; that is the great want of modern life."

When we turn back to the life and letters of those from whom we have inherited the great traditions alike of the Evangelical and of the Catholic Revival, we are startled, we are almost shocked, by the strength and severity of their language about sin. We feel that it must be exaggerated, it is so strangely unlike anything that we can bring ourselves in these days to use; and yet they had a depth, an earnestness, a steadfastness of character, a devotion to our Lord, a sense of the Divine Love, which are strangely lacking in us who speak so easily about our sins.

The truth is that man's conception of God is always coloured by his own habits of thought and feeling, and it may be that we have come to think of God as exhibiting upon a vast scale the sort of easy compassionate indulgence which we claim for ourselves and extend to others. We have isolated and exaggerated the great truth of the Fatherhood of God, robbed it of its strength and power, and concentrated ourselves only upon what is easy and comfortable to us in the thought. We have turned away, by a sort of instinct, from all that makes the New Testament what it is— stern, searching, and severe.

III. GOD AS LAW

If this be so, then plainly what we need for recovery of the sense of sin is the recovery of a truer conception of God in His relation to human life. First of all, we must learn to look upon God as *Law*.

The law of which our conscience, in its
strangely imperative voice, bears witness is
the expression of the holiness and will of a
Personal Being.   This moral law is not
something which God Himself can set aside
with a sort of large-hearted generosity.   It
is part of Himself.   It is related — and I
would ask you to remember and think upon
the phrase—of the great Bishop Butler,
that he said in his last moments, "It is an
awful thing to appear before the Moral
Governor of the World."   "The Moral
Governor of the World." We must recover
this sense of the awful source and sanctity
of the voice of conscience. To neglect or
defy its warnings, to refuse its calls, must
involve some real and inevitable retribu-
tion, because it is part of the inviolable law
of the Universe. We know the consequence
of trifling with the law of gravitation. Can
we imagine the consequences not only for
time, but for eternity, of trifling with the
moral law, of those excuses, evasions, and
silencings of conscience of which you and I
are guilty every day?

IV. GOD AS LIFE

We must recover the sense of God as *Life*. Do we really believe that true life can only be realized through union of will and mind with God? Then surely we must see in the habits which acts of sin have formed, in the tendencies within us of selfishness, of self-conceit, of jealousy, of uncharitableness, of impurity, of ambition, forces which are inevitably separating us at this moment from life, the true life in God —forces which, if they are not sternly checked and controlled may—nay, must— ultimately withdraw us wholly from Him; and to be separated from God is the outer darkness and the death.

You watch the working of a germ of disease in the human body: for a long time its influence is scarcely marked; the other members of the body discharge their functions naturally and freely; there is the full capacity of sensation, of thought, of action; but at last, and too often without

warning, the disease reaches some vital
point and all is over. In the same way our
desires, thoughts, habits of evil, may go on
for years combined with a sense of honour,
with probity of life, even with reality of
prayer and acts of communion with God;
but unless they are dealt with and controlled, sooner or later—and the pity of it
is we cannot tell when—they may reach the
vital point, and then the spirit falls from
God Who alone is its life. "The soul that
sinneth it shall die."

V. GOD AS LOVE

We must also recover the sense that God
is *Love*. "Ah!" some may say, "here we
come upon a welcome corrective to all these
harsh and gloomy thoughts. A loving God
will never allow any of His children to slip
away wholly from Him. He Who is all-
powerful and loving will surely bring all
His children back to Him." But, in truth,
a just sense of the Love of God can only

deepen the sense of sin. We dare not find
an analogy to the Love of God in the tolerant good nature, which even we know to be
an abuse of human love. We cannot ignore
the responsibility which He Himself has
entrusted to us. He will give every man
every chance which Love can justly give:
but, unless our freedom is a delusion, there
may be a chance which is the last. Nay,
let us go further and deeper. It is when
we think of what the Love of God really
means that we begin to understand the
meaning of our sin. If a child by some act
of wilfulness offends a merely indulgent
father, then from his easy tolerance the
child can learn nothing of the gravity of its
offence. But if it offends a father, part of
whose love is a high ideal to which he
yearns that the child should rise, then in
the pain on his face, in the tremor in his
voice, the child learns the meaning of its
sin. If forgiveness be given, forgiveness
which plainly cost so much is one which
must leave a deep sense of shame and sorrow, and an eager desire never to offend

again. So the Love of God which broods over each of His children is the Love of an awful Holiness—a Love which is itself a hatred of sin. If conscience fail to bring this truth home to us, then turn from conscience to the Cross of Christ. In that silent, unapproachable, awful suffering we can see the measure alike of the Love of God and of the guilt of man.

But, thanks be to God, the Cross which tells me the measure of my sin tells me also the news of my forgiveness, and it is only when I have realized the shame of the first message that I can realize the joy and wonder of the second. When I know what my sin costs the Love of God I cannot dismiss it by lightly saying, "Well, then, I will try to do better." What is there in my poor and ignorant penitence which can avail to overcome the wrath of Divine Love against my sin? What is there in my maimed and feeble will which God can accept as a sacrifice of obedience? It is when I am driven to ask these questions that I understand the wonder of the answer—

"Behold the Lamb of God which taketh away the sins of the world."

There is mystery here which I cannot fathom; but there is also satisfaction of my need which I could not have invented and which is warranted by centuries of human experience. It means that there is One, not apart from me, but joined to me by the ties of a common humanity, One in Whom I find myself, with Whose perfect sacrifice I can unite mine, poor and unworthy as it is. If my manhood is, by sincere desire and will, merged in His, then under Its shelter I can draw near to God. For He Who is the Son of Man is also Son of God—the expression of His Holy Love. Therefore, I know that in the offer which He makes to me of His own atoning sacrifice there is eternal and inviolable security. It is only when I can fall down to make the plea of "God be merciful to me a sinner" that I can rise to claim the possession of a Personal Saviour.

THE PRODIGAL SON

THE PRODIGAL SON

S. Luke xv. 11-32

I. THE GOSPEL WITHIN THE GOSPEL

WE now reach the parable which may well be called the greatest of them all. To use the true and often quoted phrase, it is *Evangelium in Evangelio* — the Gospel within the Gospel. Unerring sureness of touch and faultless simplicity of language and imagery, these we have seen to be the literary characteristics of all the parables, and in these the parable of the Prodigal Son is supreme. Regarded as a mere fragment of human literature, it is an incomparable expression of the patience and generosity with which human love bears

with and triumphs over human wilfulness
and folly. But to the Christian, who knows
Who it was Who told it, and of Whom it
was told, it is something infinitely deeper.
It is, as it were, a very sacrament of the
Eternal Love of God. Not merely are we
permitted to see in the generous love of a
human father a distant type of the attitude
of God towards His children; rather, the
Eternal Father, "of Whom every fatherhood in the world is named," speaking
through the eternal "Word," Himself
breathes through this story of the assurance
and the appeal of His own patient and all-
embracing Love. It is this, so to say, sacra-
mental presence of the Love of God in the
story which gives it its immortal power. It
is a parable to be appropriated by the spirit
rather than expounded in words. The
attempt seems vain indeed to give any new
exposition of it. The whole experience of
the Christian life for nineteen centuries is
its living commentary. We can only hope
by recalling it reverently to our minds, by
the use it may be of some fresh turn of

thought or phrase, to renew and deepen its hold upon the heart and conscience.

Doubtless it was at the moment intended to be a rebuke to the Pharisees and scribes, who had murmured, saying, "This man receiveth sinners and eateth with them!" Doubtless it had a reference to the position which the Jew and the Gentile were to take in regard to the preaching of the Gospel. It includes these temporary references, but it transcends them. It is spoken to human experience in every age. Therefore, the best method of treating it will be to unfold the response to it of our own conscience and of our own great need.

II. THE DEPARTURE FROM HOME

The younger son "said to his father, 'Father, give me the portion of thy substance that falleth to me.'" It was the craving of a false independence. He already possessed in the life of the home the full enjoyment of all his father's substance.

Speaking later to the elder son, the father expressed the abundant generosity of that home life in the words "all that is mine is thine." The son would have been right to use and enjoy that substance to the full. But he was weary of the sense of dependence: he wished to be his own master. That was the beginning of his fall. And for us— "God is our Home"; and in that home life all His gifts are freely bestowed upon us. We *can* use and enjoy them; nay, we *ought*. The marvellous endowments of our human nature—of the mind and of the senses, of love, and of beauty; all the marvels of this universe in which we live, which man half receives and half creates; these we are meant to know, to use, to enjoy. It is the very privilege of man to be able in some degree to "share God's rapture" in His creation, to see and know that it is "very good." "All that is mine is thine." We are meant to "taste the joys of life," to live in every thought and sense vividly and eagerly. "Vivens homo gloria Dei"—a living man, living to the utmost point of

intensity, is the glory of God.   But the life
is to be realized in the home—in union
with God the Father; conscious ever of His
Presence, sharing His mind, and submissive
to His Will.   It is when we wish to take
life with all its gifts and opportunities into
our own hands, and use them apart from
God, when we wish to be our own masters,
that we go wrong.   "Give me the portion
of thy substance that falleth to me"—the
making of this claim, whether in the history
of the race or of the individual man, is the
Fall.   Jesus in this parable only repeats and
vindicates in simple and homely language
the truth of an older "parable"—the story
of the first chapters of the Book of Genesis.
When in the "fretful stir" of youth, aware
of new and clamorous desires and impatient
of restraints, we say in our heart, "I will
enjoy life and have a good time in my own
way; I will be my own master," we think
that we are uttering the voice of our true
and emancipated manhood; but, alas! we
are only echoing the voice of the oldest
delusion in the world.   Some time or other

we have all made that claim; perhaps somewhere in our lives we are making it still. Every time we make it we lose our Eden. We leave "God, who is our Home."

"And he divided unto them his living." The claim is allowed. The son can take his life and use it as he pleases, if he will. God will always acknowledge His own mysterious gift of freedom. It is needless, for it is useless, to ask, why? God chose to make among His other creatures sons— beings "made in His own image"; only so from His creation could come the free love and praise and obedience which alone could satisfy that Love which is His very Life. For this great end—to use human modes of speech—He chose the risk of man's freedom. Only when we can say, "We would rather have been stones or trees or beasts than sons of God" is there any place for our complaints, and may we not add that this is something which no one who has kept any spark of his true manhood alight within him would ever dare to say. "He divided unto them his living." It is the consequence of the greatness of God's Love and of man's destiny.

III. THE SOJOURN IN THE FAR COUNTRY

The "far country," as S. Augustine tersely said, "is forgetfulness of God." It is that state of being which S. Paul described as "alienated from the life of God." There are ultimately only two states of life —the one centred in God, when it is obedient to the leading of God and is moving towards Him in thought, desire, and will; the other, centred in self, when it resists the leading of God and is moving in thought, desire, and will away from God. Between these two states most men hover to and fro, but gradually the main motive of the will— God or self—carries them to the one or to the other. In proportion as God is becoming more and more the inspiration and the goal of all our activities, we realize the

home-life for which we are made, and in
which alone we can find joy and rest.   In
proportion as that inspiration and goal are
becoming self we are taking our journey
into the far country.

True, it is not always, perhaps not often,
that a man pursues this journey recklessly
to its last stage of degradation. Messengers
of God—haunting memories of better days
and better things, the examples of better
men, rebukes of conscience, warnings in the
spirit and in the flesh—are sent to delay or
divert his course. But the parable describes
the lot of human nature, choosing self and
left to itself; and this, in order to give the
great assurance that there is no stage in that
mistaken journey from which a man cannot
make his return to God and receive His
welcome.

In interpreting the sojourn in the far
country it is, alas! easy for most of us to
use the lessons of our own experience. At
first there was the "riotous living"—the
thrill of indulged sensation, the excitement
of new and unrestricted pleasure. But soon

we learned that the resources of life were being wasted and spent, without any reward of real satisfaction. For indulgence only wears out the powers of enjoyment; it cannot satisfy them. Appetite only grows by what it feeds on. There is found to be, sooner or later, a "mighty famine," an insatiable hunger, in the far country. And the famine leads to slavery. He who set out to be his own master finds himself in the grasp of the tyrant. For there is no tyranny so lawless and pitiless as the tyranny of self-indulgence. The mere beasts are protected against the excess of their own desires by the law of instinct. But if man once parts with the rule of reason and conscience, of God, there is no such limit to restrain and protect him. He knows that he is ruining himself, but he has sold himself to a master who acknowledges no law, feels no pity, and gives no wages of reward. The money-lover must go on accumulating long after the joy of acquisition has passed away. The man of mere ambition is doomed to fretfulness, to the pains of

wounded pride, to the disease of envy, even
when he knows that the hope of success
to which he yielded himself can never
be realized.   The gambler is held in
the vice of restless excitement. The drunk-
ard becomes a sort of embodied thirst. The
sensualist, struggle as he may, is the prey
of unceasing suggestions of sin, which both
entice and torment him, and he can neither
resist nor satiate the gnawing pangs of lust.
Lastly, tied as he is, hand and foot, to his
sin, the sinner blindly obeys his master-sin,
when it sends him into every sort of degradation.   He who began by boasting "I
will go my own way" is sent to feed swine,
and is fain to fill his belly with the husks
which the swine are eating.

S. Paul, in that terrible first chapter of
the Epistle to the Romans, holds up a
flaming torch of judgment over the far
country that we may see whither it leads.
It marches with hell, for what is hell but
this slavery to insatiable sin?   "He that
is unjust, let him be unjust still; he that
is filthy, let him be filthy still."   For the

sinner, under the tyranny of his sin, "enlarges his desires as hell, and is as death, and cannot be satisfied." I can never forget the words of a poor sinner who had just escaped from her life of sin, "You need not talk about hell: I know it; I've been there for five years."

This is the Nemesis of self-indulgence, of that false craving for independence. If we can think of any part of our life which we keep for ourselves and withhold from God, it is well for us to realize that there we are setting out upon the road to a far country where recklessness, hunger, slavery, degradation, death await us. "What fruit had ye then at that time in the things whereof ye are now ashamed? For the end of these things is death."

IV. THE RETURN

At last "he came to himself." So we read of the prodigal in the parable. It is a profound word. Deep down within every

man, tossed to and fro as he may be by
the stress of his passions, there is this true
self: neglected, forsaken, yet not destroyed.
It is "the Man in men"—that image of
God in which he was made.   It is, as
R. L. Stevenson says, "the thought of
duty, the thought of something owing to
himself, to his neighbour, to his God; an
ideal of decency to which he would rise, if
it were possible, a limit of shame below
which, if it be possible, he will not stoop."
In every man, if we could but reach it, there
is this surviving remnant of the true self.
As even poor desperate Ratcliffe, in "The
Heart of Midlothian," admits, "A' body
has a conscience though it may be ill
wunnin at it."   Once won and touched, it
is true to its birth.   It remembers its Home.
We "come to ourselves" when we awake
from this miserable feverish dream-life of
sin, and realize its delusiveness and remember the real life of the Home to which in
the truth of our being we belong.   "When
he came to himself he said, How many
hired servants of my father's have bread

enough and to spare, and I perish here with hunger."

Some of us, perhaps, can understand that exclamation from our own experience. We thought, it may be, of the forces, the flowers, the birds, of Nature, the "hired servants" in the Father's House, fulfilling quietly and tranquilly the will of God, and contrasted with their peace the restlessness and disorder of our self-chosen life. Or, we thought of the dutiful faithful men we knew, and longed for their steadfast simplicity; we shrank before the conviction that we were losing touch with them, and rapidly, if only in our secret lives, identifying ourselves with the fellowship of sin; and our heart cried, "O, shut not up my soul with the sinners." Then as our thought went back to the life of the Home, it concentrated itself on the centre of it all—the Father whom we had forsaken. Then remorse, in itself only bitter and hopeless, became contrition, the pain of the soul which brings its own healing. At the remembrance of Him—

of His patient Love in contrast with our shame—a strong emotion of penitent sorrow laid hold of us, and broke the chains of slavery, and our heart's desire set free turned once again towards home. "Our soul is escaped, even as a bird out of the snare of the fowler: the snare is broken and we are delivered." "I will arise and go to my Father, and will say unto Him, Father, I have sinned."

There is but one step more, and the return is achieved. But it is a step of supreme importance. In real contrition, in sincere confession, the soul has offered its desire of return. But the will must turn that desire into act. It is just here that many a man has failed. It is not only by remorse, by sorrow, by confession, however sincere in its emotion, that we can make our escape from the far country. With the deliberate energy and concentration of the will we must rise up and leave it. "He arose and came to his Father."

V. THE RECONCILIATION

"While he was yet afar off his father saw him and was moved with compassion and ran and fell on his neck and kissed him." He was yet afar off, but he was moving towards home. The father, beholding that movement, accepts it on trust: it is the token that his son will finish the rest of the road. Therefore, even there, still afar off, he meets him, welcomes, forgives, and restores. At the sound of this twentieth verse our spirit must surely bend in adoring reverence. In it, in words which go straight to the human heart, the Almighty and Eternal Father proclaims His sovereign mercy. In heart and will and character we sinful men are afar off; our penitence, for all its reality, is imperfect; our submission is incomplete. Yet if there be in us this movement of return from self to God, from the far country to the home, God accepts it. He takes us not for what we are, but for what we are coming to be. Because of that "faith"—that homeward look of the returning spirit—we are "justified," reckoned as already returned, and accepted as sons in the generosity of forgiving love. "God commendeth His love toward us in that while we were yet sinners Christ died for us."

Do these words bring in thoughts and associations strange to the simplicity of the story? Is there any trace in it of that mysterious and perplexing doctrine of the Atonement? The question arises very naturally in our minds. But notice that the centre of the story is the experience of the prodigal, not of his father. The thoughts and the sorrows of the father's heart in these long days of his son's absence are veiled. But surely human sympathy can enable us in some degree to understand that background of the father's pain which lay behind his generous forgiveness. Ever since the day when his son had said, "Divide the portion of thy substance," the burden of rejected love must have lain heavy upon the father's soul. The news of the young man's riotous living had reached the home. In proportion to his own goodness the father's anger must have mingled with his love and sorrow. There must have been in the secret place of his mind and heart some hard-won reconciliation between his hatred of the sin and his love of the son. Doubtless in after years some knowledge of it would reach the son in his new and deeper fellowship with his father. Thus in the inner meaning of the parable the fact which is emphasized is the infinite hope for the penitent, the assurance of his forgiveness, not the cost at which in the Mind of the Holy Father it is obtained. How can we either ignore or measure the cost of forgiveness in that region of Infinite Holiness withdrawn from our sight? Some means must have been found there by which the hatred of absolute Goodness for the sin can be reconciled with the yearning of infinite Love for the sinner. We can only know what He Himself has revealed. Hints there are given to us in the words and deeds of Him who came forth from that

hidden heart of God, hints of the cost of
divine sacrifice by which man has been re-
deemed from sin and his forgiveness has
been bought.   In such wise as human
thought could grasp it, the Spirit of the
Father has revealed to His Church—His
household of returned sons—the mystery of
the cross. Reverently, if sometimes over-
confidently, the Church has tried to express
the mystery in words in a doctrine of the
Atonement. Yet the great Fact transcends
all attempts to explain it. Before that Fact
we can only bow the head in reverent penitent adoration. It is enough to know that
the Cross of Him who was Son of God and
Son of Man is alike the awful revelation of
what our sin means to the Love of God and
the welcome assurance of the fullness of
His pardon.

"And the son said unto him, Father, I
have sinned." You will notice that it is
after, not before, the embrace, that the confession comes. It is the goodness of God
that leadeth to repentance. The answering
love of the restored son can only express it-

self in his confession. In all the joy of his home-coming, in all the after-years of loyal service, the memory of that moment would remain; that heart of penitence would never become hardened. True, he no longer uses the words of which he had thought in the far country—"make me as one of thy hired servants." For he knows that he has been already welcomed as a son. But it is this very fullness of the son's heart, assured already of the Father's forgiving love, that speaks in the confession. Thus, to the Christian, the confession of his sins is no doubtful, fearful, morbid effort to extract forgiveness from an offended Taskmaster. It is the spontaneous expression of his sonship. "For ye received not the spirit of bondage again to fear, but ye received the spirit of adoption whereby we cry Abba, Father." It is that spirit of sonship which adds, "Father, I have sinned against heaven and in thy sight."

"But the father said to his servants, Bring forth quickly the best robe and put it on him." This was the father's answer to

the son's confession: the absolution was the
gift of the symbols of complete sonship. We
know with what marvellous fullness this
part of the parable has been fulfilled for us.
The life of sonship is the Life of the Perfect
Son given to us. It is with that Life by his
absolution that the penitent sinner is clothed.
The "ring" which is given, what is it but
the earnest of his inheritance, the "sealing"
of the Spirit? He is now a son in restored
right, and that Spirit of the Eternal Son
will gradually and in ever-deepening reality
fulfil the true sonship within him. The
embrace of the Father while the son was
yet a great way off—this is what S. Paul
calls "justification." The bestowal of the
gifts of sonship—this is what he calls
"sanctification." Never suppose that these
great words, in which S. Paul summarized
his own exultant experience, and which he
bequeathed to Christian thought, are only
the formulæ of barren doctrines. They are
latent here in the very heart of that parable,
which is the simplest unfolding of the
Gospel of God's Love.

"And they began to be merry." For "there is joy among the angels of God over one sinner that repenteth." We have read again this old story of the Father's forgiving Love. Does it leave us untouched—a sound of words, beautiful indeed, but signifying nothing in our own actual lives? Or does it leave us with some echo in our hearts of that "music and dancing," some hymn of praise rising from our experience as men who have known the far country and have now come home again?

VI. THE ELDER SON

This solemn question reminds us that in the parable there is one, the elder son, to whom all the joy of the household is alien, indeed repellent. If we cannot find our own experience at all interpreted by the younger son, is it possible that our place may be with the elder?

Doubtless at the moment when the parable was spoken the elder son was meant to

represent the hard, self-satisfied Pharisees
who were offended by the spectacle of a
Rabbi "receiving sinners and eating with
them." Doubtless, also, we may take him
to represent the whole race of the Jews in
its self-righteous contempt for the sinful
Gentiles. But it is possible—and more
profitable—for us to find him among the
men of our own day, or even in our own
character. Here is a man who has never
left his home: who has been faithful in the
discharge of all its duties (v. 29)—at the
moment of the prodigal's return he is at
work quietly and dutifully in the field. Is
he not typical of a very common type of
respectable and conventional religion? He
resents the disturbance of his home life by
all this fuss and noise and unusual excitement over the return of a man "who has
devoured his living with harlots." Have we
not met with him, let us say, in the decent
regular "member of the congregation" who
grumbles at the abnormal excitement and
enthusiasm of a Mission for the conversion
of the careless, or in the severely respect-

able churchwoman who "does not wish to hear about all that Rescue work among the fallen"? Truly, there is only too much of this elder-brotherly religion in our churches, and—to be quite honest—in ourselves.

Consider him, then, as he is presented here in this parable. He shares the life and work of the Home; but plainly his spirit remains hard, thankless, unsympathetic. Never has the word "Father" left his lips with that cry of personal need, that appeal of awakened love, which filled it when it was upheaved from the broken heart of the younger son in the far country. "Father" will never mean so much to him until he, too, has learned to add, "I have sinned, and am no more worthy to be called thy son." There is, indeed, no suggestion that it would be well for him also to go out into that far country and, through tasting the bitterness of its disappointments, to realize the love and peace of home. "*O felix culpa!*" is a dangerous cry. But it is in his own quiet and orderly life that he must find the proofs of his unworthiness and the need of penitence. And this will come to him if he hears in the words, "Child, thou hast ever been with me, and all that is mine is thine," the accents of a love to which his dull, self-centred life has given but a poor return. He must feel that the very order and quietness of his life has been a call to him to enter into a fellowship of special closeness and joy with his father —a call to which he has made a very grudging response. It is this humility alone which can open out the springs of his love. Again, he ought to have found in that security of the home the ground of a compassion all the more real for the prodigal who had left it; and a longing all the more earnest for his return. "I have bread enough and to spare, and he, my brother, is perishing with hunger"—if this had been his thought night and day, then even though he had never left his home he could have shared to the full the joy of the return.

This, my brother, was dead and is alive again; he was lost and is found."

Thus—to apply these thoughts—if any of

you, my readers, have by God's goodness
been kept from the sins of the far country,
if your life has not been harassed or your
flesh beset by great temptations, if your
observance of religion has been regular and
dutiful, then thank God indeed; but always
beware of the shadow of the elder brother—
the hardening of the heart.   It is the teaching of Jesus that the sins of the soul are
more grievous than the sins of the flesh:
and the sin of self-satisfaction is the most
damning of all.   Those whose lot has been
cast in quiet places, whose life has been
protected from the grosser sins, whose religion has been orderly, must keep watch
against the entry of this danger.   There are
two main defences against the elder-brotherly spirit which they must use.   The first
is—they must always keep before their consciences the infinite claims of an infinite
love. Measured by those claims, there is
no life which has not need of the prayer
"God be merciful to me a sinner."   Every
privilege possessed is only a claim for
deeper thankfulness; every point of safety

gained is to be the starting-point for a new
effort; every temptation overcome is to set
the soul free for its quest of a higher holiness; every token of God's love is to be the
call for a deeper, more self-sacrificing love
in response.   And the second defence
against the sin of the elder brother is the
charity which seeks to bring back the prodi-
gals who are wandering in the far country.
From every blessing received, we ought to
look upward in thanks to God who gave it,
and around in compassion to those who
have lost or never known it.   Those whose
life is safe and protected are just those who
are specially called to succour those whose
lives are encompassed by temptation and
harassed by struggle.   The ever present
thought of the greatness of God's Love and
the greatness of man's need—it is this, and
this alone, which can save us from the sin
of the hard and thankless heart.   "From all
hardness of heart, good Lord deliver us!"

THE LOST SHEEP

THE LOST SHEEP

S. Luke xv. 3-7 ; *S. Matt.* xviii. 12-14

I. THE SEVERITY OF THE PARABLES

THE study of the parables leaves an impression of severity upon the mind. There is scarcely one which does not contain the most solemn warnings and give rise to the most anxious searching of the heart. "The Word of God" spoken in them "is living, active, and stronger than any two-edged sword, and piercing even to the dividing of soul and spirit, of both joints and marrow, and quick to discern the thoughts and intents of the heart." Some of those which we have not been able to consider are of special severity—such as the Unmerciful

Servant, the Wicked Husbandman, the Rich Fool, and the Rich Man and Lazarus. They remind us of the truth on which Dean Church used to insist, and which we are too apt to forget, that the New Testament is a very severe book. The severity is the more remarkable because it is almost always aimed at those who consider themselves righteous or whom the world considers successful. He who becomes a disciple of Jesus enters verily a stern school. Yet, like the sunlight breaking through the clouds, even in the parables we see the light of the divine love breaking through the severity of the divine judgment. It shines full and clear in the last parable of which we thought, the Prodigal Son: and lest the impression left on our minds should be too stern, I would close our study of the parables by choosing one, short indeed and simple, yet glittering as a jewel with the light of divine compassion—the parable of the Lost Sheep.

II. THE ETERNAL COMPASSION

"What man of you having a hundred
sheep, and having lost *one* of them, doth not
leave the ninety and nine?" The contrast
of the numbers—ninety and nine and one—
is only meant to heighten the emphasis laid
on the importance in the eyes of the
shepherd of the *one* that was lost. To us,
familiar as we are with the masses of people
gathered especially in our great cities,
wandering through all the sins and sorrows,
the hopes and fears, the love and labour of
human life "as sheep without a shepherd,"
it is more natural to think of leaving the
one in safety to seek the ninety and nine that
are lost. But that is not our Lord's point.
He wishes simply to bring out the care of
the shepherd for each single sheep. More
and more, as we grow in care for our own
life and for the lives of our fellows, we
learn to stay ourselves upon the great truth
—that God's knowledge and love of each
single soul is *absolute*. "Are not five sparrows sold for two farthings? and not one of

them is forgotten in the sight of God. But
the very hairs of your head are all num-
bered. Fear not: ye are of more value than
many sparrows." It is of all truths the
most certain: for God would not be God
unless it were true. He would not be
infinite in knowledge or love unless He
knew with absolute completeness and loved
with absolute intensity every single soul.
And it is of all truths the most sustaining.
It means that any solitary soul who at any
time and in any part of the world has wandered from its true good is marked and
missed and wanted by Almighty God.
Place yourself in imagination in the centre
of a great city, say in a crowded street in
East London, watch the stream of lives,
toil-worn and anxious, or noisy and light-
hearted, as it flows past you; note the children, on whose faces the coming shadows
have not yet fallen, the laughing lads and
girls keeping the shadows at bay by the
boisterousness of their animal spirit, the
working men and harassed women with
their looks of either good-humoured pati-

ence or sullen endurance: think of all the histories of love and hope, of struggle and sorrow which lie behind these fleeting faces, half hidden by them and half revealed. Is there not here a pathos which would be too poignant in its appeal unless one's own answering pity were but a feeble reflection of the infinite pity in the heart of the Eternal? Imagine, somewhere withdrawn from this busy scene, in a garret perhaps in some back street, a young girl tasting alone the bitterness of the dregs of that cup of sin which when she first put it to her lips was bright and sparkling. Then remember that this single strayed child of His is to the Eternal God as the one sheep that was lost to the watchful shepherd.

To think of our own lives—have there not been moments in the experiences of most of us when the sense of loneliness was borne in upon the soul—the sense that, after all, our life stands apart, its burden of sin or sorrow or longing unknown and unshared by others? These are the very moments when faith can reveal to us one eye that sees, one heart that understands, one hand that touches with sympathy and strength—the eye, the heart, the hand of the Eternal Compassion. To God everything in this universe, from the flower in the open field to the human soul in the mysteries of love and pain, is known both in its relation to all other things and in its own separate significance; and in each aspect known with a perfect knowledge which is one with a perfect love. If there is a God at all, we cannot believe less. Since there is a God, need we ask for more? Yet it is more that He gives.

III. THE SHEPHERD SEEKS

"What man of you having a hundred sheep, and having lost one of them, doth not . . . *go after* that which is lost?" We might conceive of a perfect knowledge which marks the wandering of a human soul as it marks the failure of a stunted tree—all-knowing and all-indifferent. We might even conceive of a vast love (we

could scarcely call it perfect) which feels
the pity of the wandering, and yet in its
serene hold upon the mysterious wisdom of
a plan which involves the freedom of man
leaves the wanderer alone. But God's Incarnation in Jesus the Saviour reveals to us
infinite knowledge, and love, not merely
marking and missing, but going after the
soul that has strayed. It reveals the coming
forth of the Eternal Companion to seek and
to save that which is lost. Man knows in
his conscience that he has wandered. The
restlessness of his heart, the inevitable sigh
which rises from it when in a moment of
quiet he reviews the story of his life, betray
that knowledge. "We have erred and
strayed like lost sheep: we have followed
too much the devices and desires of our
own hearts." That after all is man's verdict
on himself when he brings his life to the
court of conscience. He can judge, but he
cannot redeem himself. He knows that he
has wandered, but he cannot compass his
own return. It is then that, looking up to
the immutable heavens and feeling dimly

that behind them lies surely some heart that
knows and cares, he cries, "Oh that there
might come forth from this vast and distant
Power some visible Messenger of its compassion, some divine Assistant of men, to
recall them from their wandering and bring
them back to the truth."   And, in answer,
"See the Christ stand!"

It was a true and touching sign of the
need of man's heart, of the welcome which
it gave to God's answer, that the early
Christians loved to imagine and pourtray
their Redeemer as the strong and kindly
Shepherd.   On their gems and seals and
household ornaments, on the tombs in
which they laid their dead who seemed to
have wandered to "the land where all
things are forgotten," they imprinted the
likeness of the Shepherd.   Since they were
still, as it were, in the bright early morning
of their redemption, they loved to represent
him as a shepherd blithe and strong and
beautiful.   As it was the image of this Good
Shepherd which was the first to attract and
express the grateful love of the Christian

Church, so is it not this same image that we would wish to have before our eyes at the last, when we, too, set forth upon our dim journey, lost to sight, along the untrodden ways of death? "The Lord is my Shepherd; therefore can I lack nothing. Yea, though I walk through the valley of the shadow of death, I will fear no evil: for Thou art with me; Thy rod and Thy staff comfort me." How can we measure the difference to the world and to our own life since we have had the vision of Jesus as the Shepherd who "goes after" the sheep that is lost?

IV. THE SHEPHERD FINDS

"He goes after that which is lost *until he find it.*" When the shepherd has gone forth nothing daunts him, nothing stops his course: he goes on until he finds. Before the Good Shepherd who came forth on that first Christmas morning, as He lay in His mother's arms, what a weary stretch of

travelling lay! The journeyings to and fro
wherein "the Son of Man had not where to
lay his head," the long vigils on the mountains, the weariness and disappointment, the
betrayal by His disciples, the agony in the
garden, the shame of Calvary, and that last
and awful desert void of the very sense of
the Father's presence, from which the cry
rose, "My God, my God, why hast Thou
forsaken me?" The seeker had gone so far
that He was, as it were, identified with the
pain of the lost. He made all that long
journey so that no one lost anywhere in the
desert of sin or sorrow should ever doubt
but that the Shepherd was at hand Who
had gone after him until He found him.
There is no distance from which by the
power of His redeeming grace we may not
make our return to God.

There is, indeed, one limit, though only
one, which the Good Shepherd Himself
cannot overpass—it is the limit of man's
own consent to be found and restored. He
cannot find the soul which to the end, in
spite of all His seeking, says, "I will not

have Thee." We dare not assert, whatever we may dare to hope, there will be no one "finally lost." All we can say—is it not enough?—is that whatever infinite Love can do to bring back every single wanderer will be done. Can we not trust to the uttermost a Love which showed the measure of its longing on the Cross?

V. THE SHEPHERD REJOICES

"And when he hath found it, he layeth it on his shoulders, rejoicing. And when he cometh home, he calleth together his friends and neighbours, saying unto them, Rejoice with me, for I have found my sheep which was lost. I say unto you that even so there shall be joy in heaven over one sinner that repenteth." This word of Jesus—"I say unto you," I who know as none other knows—is a welcome token that there is no impassible barrier between our world of difficulty and doubt, of long struggle and wistful aspiration, of failures

and of shadows, and that eternal world of
Reality and Truth, of Rest and Achieve-
ment, where the will of God is ever done.
There is knowledge there of our struggles
and mistakes, joy there at the sight of any
human life, after many wanderings,
brought back to the truth. We are, even
when we seem to be most alone, "encompassed about with a great cloud of wit-
nesses." In that world, where the atmosphere is Truth itself, things are seen in
their true proportions: joy is found in the
things that are truly joyful. It is a wonderful thought that even we can cause this "joy
in heaven": and that we do so not by our
successes, our wealth, and our fame, but by
that penitence with which in the secrecy of
our souls we respond to the seeking Son of
God, and allow Him to find us and bring
us back to Himself. But here we reach a
region where it is best to think in silence.